WHAT OTHEF

MW00358917

Stop Trying to Fix Me: I'm Grieving As Fast As I Can is the unflinching personal experience of a widow who is just now beginning to emerge from profound grief some two years after her husband's death. Clark shares what it has been like to experience his rapidly declining health, the death itself, and the two years since his death-what she has found helpful and what has increased her sense of grief and isolation. She reminds readers that each person's grief is unique to them, including the process of healing itself and how long it takes until they begin to have a glimpse of resuming life without their loved one. Her earlier near-death experience and profound spiritually-transformative experience have supported her in the grieving process in that she is certain of life-after-death, but they do not blunt the raw pain of missing a life-long love. Experiences of after-death communication from her deceased husband have contributed to her healing process as well.

She has courageously written of her loss in the midst of the loss, not from the vantage point of someone who is writing about the memory of a loss. From that perspective, her writing will be especially helpful to people who are currently undergoing overwhelming grief. One of the most helpful things we can experience when we are in the midst of grief is to hear the personal story of someone who is working through her grief and beginning to see a glimpse of hope for the future. Nancy Clark is that companion on the journey and I recommend this book not only to bereaved loved ones, but also to counselors, friends and people with near-death experiences and spiritually-transformative experiences as they strive to be helpful to bereaved people in their lives."

—Pam Kircher, MD
Author of *Love is the Link: A Hospice Doctor Shares her Experience of Near-Death and Dying*
www.pamkircher.com

"The death of a spouse after a long loving marriage can be and often is devastating to the survivor. It leaves an open wound that cannot be cauterized, and certainly not by formulaic well-meaning words intended either to comfort or to change the subject away from the survivor's unbearable, unrelenting grief. Nancy Clark has had to endure both her grief and the sometimes almost heartless attempts of others to "cure her of her sorrow." This is her moving and searingly honest testimony that shows that while grief may someday at least subside, the love that animates it only grows stronger. Nancy's grief is a kind of sacred remembrance, a way of honoring that love until both she and her beloved can be united again. Why, then, should one try to overcome it? It is not an illness to be cured, but a means of cherishing the unfathomable beauty of an undying love."

—Kenneth Ring, Ph.D.
Author of Lessons from the Light

"This unique book offers a wealth of information about grief and after-death communication (ADC) experiences. I recommend it very highly to everyone who is providing emotional support to someone who is grieving the death of a loved one. I wish it had been available when many of my family members and friends had died."

—Bill Guggenheim,
Co-author of *Hello From Heaven*

"I have lived what Nancy writes about and know that only love is immortal. Because of the difficulties people have dealing with loss and death we are unprepared when it comes into our lives. Only you can fix yourself and heal your wounds and life but Nancy's experience and words can help to coach and guide you through this difficult time."

—Bernie Siegel, MD
Author of *Buddy's Candle and Faith, Hope & Healing*

Stop Trying to Fix Me: I'm Grieving As Fast As I Can is a beautiful testament to the fact that love is truly eternal. Nancy Clark takes readers on an incredible journey through love and loss as she grieves the passing of her husband Ched. She helps us to understand that each person's grieving process is unique and should be respected as such.

"Nowhere in history will the same thoughts be going on in anyone's mind, soul and spirit," she writes. "Grieving is unique to everyone going through it and it is important that we don't compare our reactions to another's, or one person's pain to another's. We all hurt when we face the death of a loved one. Pain is pain, no matter how it looks on the outside. We need to express our grief in a way that feels most real to us."

Death is not the end. It is a continuous journey of the soul and when we are willing and ready, it will lead us to live purposely. It will eventually bring us to a new beginning, a new life."

—Josie Varga,
Author of *Visits from Heaven and Visits to Heaven*

"Nancy Clark is an amazing 'earth-angel' and you'll want to benefit from her wisdom. She emanates love and light in her writing and her life. I'm more psychic when she's around and, on two occasions, I've seen her high inner energy affect electronic device functioning. This book will help heal those who are grieving and guide those who are trying to help them."

—Mark Pitstick, MA, DC,
Author of *Soul Proof* and *Radiant Wellness*

Stop Trying To Fix Me:
I'm Grieving As Fast As I Can

Nancy Clark

Stop Trying to Fix Me: I'm Grieving As Fast As I Can

Nancy Clark

Copyright © Nancy Clark 2013

Published by 1stWorld Publishing
P.O. Box 2211, Fairfield, Iowa 52556
tel: 641-209-5000 • fax: 866-440-5234
web: www.1stworldpublishing.com

First Edition

LCCN: 2013947578

SoftCover ISBN: 978-1-4218-8674-9

All rights reserved. No part of this book may be reproduced or utilized in any form or by any means, electronic or mechanical, including photocopying or recording, or by any information storage and retrieval system, without permission in writing from the author.

This material has been written and published for educational purposes to enhance one's wellbeing. In regard to health issues, the information is not intended as a substitute for appropriate care and advice from health professionals, nor does it equate to the assumption of medical or any other form of liability on the part of the publisher or author. The publisher and author shall have neither liability nor responsibility to any person or entity with respect to loss, damages or injury claimed to be caused directly or indirectly by any information in this book.

With love to Ched, my sons, Chris and Randy,

and to the One who brought us all together.

CONTENTS

Acknowledgments

I wish to thank those individuals who were not trying to "fix me" by lecturing me, those who were not judgmental, those who were not trying to minimize my loss, or put a timeline on my loss.

I am grateful to the ones who were supportive and cared about my feelings. I am thankful to the ones who could admit that they couldn't make it better for me. I am appreciative of my friends who gave me a hug and said not a word to me because there are no words. I am thankful for my friends who took me to dinner to celebrate my birthday.

I am deeply grateful to my dear friend Kenneth Ring, Ph.D, world-renowned near-death experience researcher and author, for his support during those days when I experienced such raw grief that overwhelmed me at times and for his encouragement to write this book. When I asked him for his honest evaluation of my manuscript, his opinion and suggestions on how to improve it were especially helpful to me. I will always hold a special place in my heart for him.

Bill Guggenheim noted author, *Hello From Heaven!* deserves my immeasurable gratitude for his gracious and endearing spirit. His invaluable insights and support about grief and mourning coupled with his editorial assistance on my manuscript helped to make a significant contribution to this book. My gratitude for his kindness goes beyond words.

My editor, Celie Thomas, was a God-send to me. All her comments throughout my manuscript alerting me to the corrections that needed to be made were invaluable to me.

I owe my deep gratitude to Bernie Siegel, M.D.; Kenneth Ring, Ph.D.; Bill Guggenheim; Pam Kircher, M.D.; Josie Varga; and Mark Pitstick, D.C. for believing that my book was worthy of their endorsements, and to my publisher, Rodney Charles, 1st World Publishing.

Eben Alexander, M.D., best-selling author, *Proof of Heaven*, was especially supportive to me during the initial phase of my grief, and his kindness must be acknowledged. We both had near-death experiences, and Eben was there for me in that special way. He never faltered in his belief that I could offer something back to others.

I am indebted to my psychologist friend, Randy Snyder, Ph.D, who was the first one to contact me as my world was falling apart right before my eyes. His counsel provided me with a crutch to lean upon when I felt like my limbs could no longer support me. I am forever in his debt.

My dear friends Mark Lutz and Pat Stillisano, are friends that every person should be blessed with. They have been there for me through every joy and sorrow of my life for so many years, and they have demonstrated an enduring faith in the mission that I have: to induce spirituality back into people's personal lives. I am so grateful for their support and their love.

I deeply appreciate my friends, Joyce Gibb, RN, Jeff Lutz, David Lang, and PMH Atwater for their generous support.

The members of the Columbus, Ohio International Association for Near-Death Studies, (IANDS), were always loving and supporting me. I have treasured their friendships enormously.

Vernon Sylvest, M.D., is a cherished friend who has supported me, prayed for me and someone who unselfishly gave so much to me. We have shared the miraculous, the inexplicable, and the inspirational in our work together.

I must acknowledge a very special thank you to my sons Chris and Randy for their quiet strength and counsel that have been a true blessing to me. They are the embodiment of joy that has enabled me to put my life back together again. They inherited the best of their father's traits. Even when my own life is over, I will continue to love them for eternity.

Last but not least, I thank God whose love for me strengthens me, encourages me, and will eventually heal my grief. Thank you for giving me this life and something wonderful to do with it.

Why I Wrote This Book

Love is the most powerful and indescribable force in the universe. When you love someone you feel connected to them in such a way that the heart, mind, and soul have been expanded in size to be beyond measure.

My husband and I were together for over 50 years. In all that time, we gave to one another without hesitation, without question, without regret, and without second thought, our enduring love to one another. With that love came indescribable caring, understanding, and selflessness, comfort, and the assuring knowledge that we were meant to share our lives with one another until "death do us part."

On March 9, 2011, Ched died. He was 71 years old. What followed was my personal journey through the process of bereavement to find the hope that I could continue living my life without him. It is a story that I think will help others to experience that same hope when they, themselves, are suddenly thrust into a similar passage into a new and different life without their loved one. In some way, I can be here for them.

Grief responses are as individualized as each individual person, and one's sorrow needs individual expression. It can be intensely devastating or in some cases repressed, awaiting expression in some unhealthy manner such as resorting to drugs or alcohol, prolonged depression, or anything that becomes severe enough to impact daily living.

Grieving is not new to me. You don't get to be my age without having lost your parents, grandparents, all your aunts and uncles, and dear friends. My mother and I were extremely close; we were like twins. When she died, I grieved of course. Who wouldn't? But my grief did not last long. It seemed I was able to move on with my life within a reasonable time frame. But with the death of my husband, my journey through grief was like a vile of poison to my soul. Some aspects of my grief were agonizing while others were bearable.

Human beings have a remarkable ability to respond to the needs of others. Crisis events such as tornadoes, floods, bombings, and deaths bring out the best in people and give us the opportunity to open our hearts to engage in compassion, our capacity to put our love into action.

Even so, after Ched died, many of my friends didn't know what to say or do. Some made remarks that hurt me instead of comforting me. They wanted to lecture me or give me advice on how to stop missing Ched. The intent of course, was to help me to stop grieving. But of course I knew that no one could fix me or take my grief away. I had to move through the grief process in my own way and in my own time.

Many people rely on their faith or spirituality to help them diminish their feelings of grief by believing that life after death exists. This belief can be extremely comforting to those whose loved one has died. I don't "believe in" life after death. I KNOW it exists because I died during childbirth and went to be with God whose unconditional love is beyond description. I returned from that near-death experience to know that consciousness survives after the body ceases to function. Years later, another near-death-like experience occurred and forever transformed my life. I was sent back from Heaven's door to speak and write what my Great Teacher, the Light of God revealed to me during those moments spent with God. My passion is to bring hope to those who question whether life is a continuum or not. I have also included information in this book about after-death communications which support evidence that these amazing stories are precious gifts from our loved ones to let us know they are still with us in spirit.

I have learned through my life and through Ched's death that love never dies. Love is always with me, sustaining me through all the trials and joys of my life. For me personally, it is God's love – that Divine power – which will ultimately bring me gentle peace and enfold me with the strength to walk forward into a new life.

Even when I feel the devastating heartache of missing Ched, I still have the hope and faith that I can emerge from this nightmare and survive this ordeal. Without that hope, life would be wretched. I realize that my life is a new beginning whether I like it or not, and as dark gives way to dawn, I shall follow my heart through the many changes I will be going through, knowing that love will always guide my way. I am never alone – and neither is anyone else!

My wish in writing this book is, in part, to convey a loving emotional connection that can help others who are experiencing their own grief, and seeking perspective when it is hard to come by. This is my story and how I am dealing the cards that life has dealt me. I want to pass along what I have learned. I hope it helps.

Nancy Clark

1

Love For a Lifetime

"True love begins in heaven's bower, unfolds on earth a perfect flower."

—Ardelia Cotton Barton, *Love's Language*

"Who is that boy?" I asked my girlfriend while we were seated in our high school gymnasium watching all the boys walking into the gym to practice for our school's annual Sports Night competition events. "He's the new boy in school," she said. "He came from a military academy prep school in Virginia." My heart fluttered and I knew Cupid's arrow had just pierced my heart. One could immediately tell there was something different about this boy as he walked into the gym with the other boys. This boy held his shoulders back, chin tucked in, chest out just like the military requires. As for the other boys marching into the gym, well shall I say, they looked quite the opposite. They looked like this was the last place they wanted to be as they dragged their feet across the gym floor, heads drooping to avoid the girls' stares.

The year was 1958. I was a junior and Ched was a senior who had just transferred to our high school from Hargrave Military Academy in Chatham, Virginia a week earlier. After I learned a little about him from my girlfriend, I soon discovered that all the girls in school were talking about him. He was the center of attention, mine included.

Every Saturday night our high school held a dance called "Canteen." Rock and Roll was that era's favorite music to dance to, and Canteen was where everyone wanted to be on a Saturday night. Boys were on one side of the room always checking out the girls who were on the other side of the room while the girls awaited that tap on the shoulder from a boy asking her to dance. I remember that Al Hibbler's "Unchained Melody" played over the loudspeaker, a song so dreamy, everyone rushed onto the dance floor to slow dance. I was standing on the sidelines talking to my girlfriend when I felt a tap on my shoulder. "Would you like to dance?" I heard a male voice ask me. I turned around to see who it was. It was the new boy in school!

While we were dancing, my heart was beating so fast and I was trembling from nervousness. "Would you like to go out after the dance with me and grab a pizza with some of the other students?" he asked.

Oh no! The new boy in school that all the girls were swooning over wanted me to go out with him after the dance and I couldn't go out with him.

"I'm sorry but I can't. I drove my car tonight and I brought some friends with me. I have to drive them home. I'm sorry, but I can't." I replied.

I was devastated! "Now he will never ask me out again because I turned him down," I thought. But a week later, he called and asked me if I would like to go on a double-date to the movies. I was ecstatic and I accepted.

Several years after we were married, Ched told me that at the time of our first double-date to the movies, his friend had asked Ched's ex-girlfriend to go on that double-date with us. Ched didn't know who his friend's date was until we all met up with one another. I could only imagine how Ched must have felt that night but he never let on to me that his ex-girlfriend was with us that evening. We all had a great time, but I was clueless as to what Ched and his ex-girlfriend must have been feeling.

However, I did notice that when I entered my history class Monday morning after our Saturday night date, Ched's ex-girlfriend was surrounded by her friends and they were all giving me icy stares and were talking about me. Again, I was clueless and simply brushed off their chilly frowns.

Ched and I have been together ever since that first date, through high school, through college, through forty-nine blessed years of marriage, his illness, and yes, even through his death.

Ched told me when he asked me to dance that evening at Canteen that he fell in love with me at that moment, just as I did with him. I believe that some people are meant to be together and the universe has a way of bringing them together. It was a blessed life we shared – a marriage made in Heaven with the two of us sharing abiding love for a lifetime!

Through our deep love for one another we created two wonderful sons who, to this day, remind me so much of their father's values – honesty, integrity, wisdom, faithfulness and love – the hallmarks of a soul weaving together a multifaceted, purposeful life.

Being fully immersed in the day-to-day matters that made up our lives together as a family, there was always the understanding that we were the anchors of great love for one another. Our roots went deep into the pit of our hearts and while we occasionally felt like we were falling through the cracks of life, our love provided the solid ground on which to land. We had a foundation that sometimes challenged us yet kept us learning and growing honestly and fearlessly. This God-given gift took us both by the hand and introduced us to a way of life that taught us the meaning of the words, "I will love you no matter what."

We had no formula for marriage and raising a family. We simply allowed the moments of our lives to teach us and guide us, rather than simply reacting to them. It was a very good life and we were blissfully happy.

"Life's greatest happiness is to be convinced we are loved."

—Victor Hugo, *Les Miserables*

Living and Dying On His Own Terms

Ched lived and died on his own terms. He loved to eat and with me being a gourmet cook, he ate more than he was supposed to. Moderation was not in his vocabulary. He gained weight but wouldn't exercise. When he was diagnosed with diabetes, I learned everything about the disease and how to manage his care. I would calculate every morsel of food I prepared for him so he would keep his blood sugar levels in balance. Little did I know that when he went to the office, he would eat the doughnuts and munch on all the candy that were on one of the conference tables. Sometimes he would go out for lunch instead of eating what I prepared for him, and he would order high fat grilled Reuben sandwiches. After dinner he would raid the refrigerator and eat more.

He didn't seem to care what he was doing to his body; he enjoyed his food and he would often tell me, "I want to enjoy my life, not feel deprived."

But I would tell him that he was endangering his health and he would develop complications of diabetes if he didn't lose the weight and watch his blood sugars. I would tell him that he was shortening his life. His reply was always the same: "You have to die sometime and while I am living, I want to enjoy my life."

It didn't matter what I said. He was going to enjoy one of life's pleasures for him by eating whatever he wanted. Besides, when someone is thinking along those lines, they think they are invincible and wouldn't get the complications of the disease he had. He was always the optimist.

Well, it finally caught up with him after some years of neglecting his health. His kidneys shut down and he had to go on kidney dialysis to remove the build-up of toxins from his body. He developed heart disease, seizures, and many other health issues. We went to the hospital over 100 times during his illness.

Kidney dialysis changes a person's life and it changes the spouse's life as well. Ched could no longer drive so I had to drive him the half hour to the dialysis center and wait the five long hours in the waiting room with the other wives during treatments. We did this three times a week for five years.

My friends would ask me how I managed to care for Ched during his illness. "This must be so much stress for you Nancy, I couldn't do it," they would tell me.

I was always puzzled by those comments. Stress? I couldn't relate to that. I always felt it was an honor and a privilege to take care of Ched. I drove him everywhere to his doctors' appointments and took notes so we wouldn't forget what we were being told. I washed his behind and changed his clothes when he had diarrhea accidents. I comforted him during his seizures. I rubbed his back when his spinal stenosis flared up. I got up in the middle of the night when his leg cramps were so severe he would writhe in pain while I tried to work the muscle cramp out. When he vomited I cleaned it up. I helped him walk with his walker. I fed him when he couldn't. When he fell, I helped him to stand up again. So many caregiver responsibilities were performed with love because that's the only thing I ever felt for him.

He would ask me if I knew then what I know now, would I have married him? Without hesitation, I said a resounding YES!!! And I meant that from the bottom of my heart. To this day, I most certainly would do it all over again, in a loving heartbeat.

"Being deeply loved by someone gives you strength, while loving someone deeply gives you courage."

—Lao Tzu

I believe our souls know when it is time to leave this earthly realm. One morning during the summer of 2010 we were having our usual morning coffee together at the kitchen table located next to the floor to ceiling sliding glass door. We loved our morning ritual being together like that. It was just the two of us enjoying those quiet moments without the sensory disruption of television or any other external stimuli to distract from our quality time together.

The morning dew on the grass seemed to sparkle like clear gems; the trees in the forest stood tall with an air of grandeur. Ched had finished counting the number of different bird species that flew into the bird feeder when he suddenly said, "I will probably be dead by this time next year."

I looked into his eyes and his gaze was contemplative as if he were lost in thought. I didn't want to embrace the idea that what he was saying might be true. I paused in silence as I listened to the deep-seated wisdom of my soul that hinted to me that what he was saying was true. I didn't say anything to him. Perhaps in retrospect, I should have. Perhaps that was an opportunity for the both of us to speak to each other directly about this balance between the conscious and the unconscious minds that spoke to both of us that morning. Perhaps if we had taken the time to tune into our feelings and be honest about them, I could have moved through my defense mechanism that was mixed with feelings of fear and avoidance.

As it turned out, Ched died on March 9, 2011 just six months from our conversation that morning.

Everyone who has experienced the loss of a loved one has a story to tell, and each person's story is unique. No two people share the same life experiences, events or reactions, and it is important to allow people to share their stories. It helps to dissipate the tremendous pain that takes place during the grief process and reinforces that one's loss matters. I also believe it is an opportunity for others to feel and experience their own compassion as they listen to the story being shared by the grieving person, thus, holding enormous value for both the story-teller and the listener. This is my story.

For the time being, it is important to understand that grief is all about rebuilding ourselves from the ground up. It is hard to "let go" of our perceptions and beliefs and our resistance to the emptiness that our grief unmasks. Taking that first step into the void is downright scary, but it is also a realm of possibilities to move forward toward wholeness. I didn't have this wisdom during the initial stage of my grief. I felt that my emotional pain was so immense that I would never be able to survive living with that kind of pain. I couldn't believe that others who went through their grief journey talked of an eventual acceptance of the death of their loved one. *Who in their right mind could accept this nightmare?* I wondered.

I have come to realize that I must give my grief its time and go through it in my own way. No one can complete this painful journey for me. No one can "fix" me. I'm grieving as fast as I can!

2

The Beginning of the End

How does one become a butterfly? she asked pensively. You must want to fly so much that you are willing to give up being a caterpillar."

—Trina Paulus

On December 29, 2010 while on the kidney dialysis machine, Ched developed sudden, severe abdominal pain. I drove him to the ER after he was disconnected from the dialysis machine. He was lucid, even suggesting that we should stop at a fast-food restaurant to grab a burger before we got to the hospital.

"No!" I said. "You are going to the ER for a diagnosis; they will run tests and you should not have anything in your stomach."

I was determined that he would not have anything to eat before we got to the hospital. He was irritated with me but since I was driving, he couldn't get his darn burger! We talked during our drive and it was clear to me that his mental faculties were sharp. In fact, when he was first getting hooked up to the dialysis machine that morning, the nurse asked Ched, as usual, to do her math calculations. She needed to know the different percentages of solutions to administer in the dialysis machines for the patients.

Ched was very intelligent and he could do accurate math calculations in his head thus, saving time for the nurse having to figure it out on paper. He did those calculations that morning prior to developing his severe abdominal pain and he was his usual self, talking and laughing with the nurses. I am relaying this important information because in a moment you will understand why.

We arrived at the hospital and very quickly, the doctors evaluated him. He had developed an air bubble in his portal vein. As soon as the diagnosis was made, a flurry of nurses and doctors entered the room. No one said a word to me; they were too busy attending to Ched, removing the monitors that were connected to him and preparing to remove the bed he was lying in to another room.

A rather subdued physician entered the room while this flurry of activity was going on and he stood next to me without saying a word. He kept looking at Ched with what appeared to be grave concern for him. I became worried at that point.

"Doctor, please tell me what is happening," I demanded.

The doctor said quietly so Ched would not hear his words. "Your husband has developed an air bubble in his portal vein. We are going to transfer him to ICU so we can monitor him better."

That was all he told me but I needed more information.

"What is air in his portal vein?" I asked the doctor.

Again, quietly and with great concern on his face, he said, "It's a very serious condition."

"How serious?" I asked.

He was quiet. He didn't answer my question. But his face spoke the words I did not want to hear but yet, I needed to hear. So once again, I turned to him and asked him a direct question.

"Can my husband die from this?"

"Yes." He replied. "That's why we are moving him to ICU in the event anything happens. Should something go wrong, it will happen very quickly and we won't have time to move him into ICU at that time. We are preparing for the worst case scenario at this time."

All of a sudden my mind was going in all directions at the same time. *What do you mean my husband can die? No, he can't die! This isn't happening! Oh God, don't let Ched die!* My thoughts were frenzied and horrified!

I accompanied Ched, the doctors and nurses as we raced through the halls to ICU. I couldn't accept the fact that my beloved could die at any moment. I wasn't ready for this. I kept my eyes focused on Ched who was unaware of his diagnosis or the severity of this situation and my love for him poured out of my heart and into his. I thought perhaps my love for him would be the miracle that would save his life so I just kept praying for him as we sped toward the ICU unit.

Although Ched was still in severe abdominal pain, he was still lucid, joking around with the doctors and nurses, and giving them accurate past medical history information. Then he began to have very slight seizure activity. The type seizures Ched had are called myoclonic type seizures. They are not the usual ones you may be familiar with called grand mal seizures.

With myoclonic type seizures, the muscles are affected and they twitch sometimes lasting an hour, even a day or longer. Usually Ched's symptoms would begin with slurred speech as the facial muscles would begin to tighten and twitch. Gradually, his entire body would become affected. Sometimes the seizures would stop spontaneously, other times we had to go to the ER. The usual treatment for this type of seizure was to give Ched an IV injection of Ativan in the ER which would relax the myoclonic type seizure activity. We were accustomed to this treatment for years and it always worked.

When Ched was being seen in the ICU for air in his portal vein and he was just starting to have a very mild episode of the seizure, I told the doctor who attended to him that his seizures had always been treated with Ativan and he just needed an IV injection of that drug to stop the oncoming seizure in its tracks.

A New Drug

The doctor said he wanted to call in a neurologist rather than dispensing the Ativan himself. When the neurologist came, I explained the type of seizures Ched suffered from and the type of treatment he received for them. Ched also explained to the neurologist how those seizures affected his body and that Ativan was the usual treatment that always alleviated those symptoms. The neurologist then said he didn't like Ativan, he was going to give Ched a different anti-seizure medication instead. Within 2 hours after injection of this particular drug, Ched's brain was fried! He was no longer lucid. He was hallucinating, he didn't know where he was; he said his birthday was in 2017 but then corrected himself and said, "No, that's Nancy's birthday."

Confused, I couldn't understand what was happening to Ched. *What was causing his cognitive abilities to be so suddenly diminished? Was this condition something associated with air in his portal vein?* I wondered.

"Doctor, why is Ched hallucinating?" I asked the attending physician.

"I don't know why." he replied.

The neurologist left as soon as he gave the injection of the anti-seizure medication so I couldn't ask him the questions that I was posing to the doctors who came to check on Ched's condition. My sons and I were left with no answers.

Ched had to have surgery the next day to remove the air

bubble in his portal vein but when they opened him up, they discovered the air bubble had dissipated on its own. That was very good news. He was out of danger. Now all he had to do was recuperate from the surgery. But his brain was still fried! The doctors could not figure out what was causing this. He was hallucinating most of the time, with infrequent episodes of lucidity.

I kept asking the doctors if the neurologist's injection of the anti-seizure drug caused this condition with Ched but I was always told, "I don't know." For the entire 16 days Ched was in the hospital, that neurologist never came to check on him or take him off that anti-seizure drug. Why this neurologist administered and kept him on this drug baffled me. Ched had never been prescribed a long-term anti-seizure medication for daily use. As I said earlier, whenever he would have a seizure, the ER doctor would administer an IV injection of Ativan and in a few hours, his seizure subsided and he was fine.

I told the attending physician several times, "Please have the neurologist speak with me because I would like to know what is happening to Ched's brain."

Each time I made that request I was told that a call was made to the neurologist and he would call me. But he never called me. I wanted Ched to be taken off that anti-seizure drug but the doctors would not remove it, telling me that it was a tricky drug to withdraw and they weren't trained to wean him off it, and that it was better left to the neurologist to do that. But the neurologist never sent an order to wean him off it nor did he visit Ched to evaluate him! I was so frustrated trying to get the other doctors to take him off that drug. No one was listening to me. As far as they were concerned, this wasn't their specialty and they wanted it left up to the neurologist to deal with since he administered the drug.

My husband wasn't eating anything since he was admitted to the hospital. At first I understood that his condition probably couldn't tolerate food, but as the days went by, I noticed they were not bringing any food for him. I began to get worried. On day 10 of his hospital stay, I kept asking the nurse why they weren't giving him any food.

I asked the nurse specifically if they could give him IV nourishment and was told, "He's not at that stage yet."

"What stage is that?" I asked. "He needs some kind of nourishment; he's getting weaker by the day." I replied. "Please ask the doctor to give him some nourishment," I said.

The nurse left the room somewhat annoyed by my request. She came back a few minutes later and told me that an order was sent to the dietician to evaluate Ched. She quickly left the room. A sense of relief came over me. Ched wasn't able to speak for himself, so I had to be his voice. But sometimes I thought no one was listening to what I was saying.

Two days passed and no dietician came to see Ched. The next day I happened to see the dietician in the hall coming from another patient's room so I went out into the hall and spoke with her. She told me that no order had been sent to her to evaluate Ched. *Oh God! What is happening? Why is my husband being treated this way?* I pleaded with her to evaluate Ched because he had been without any nourishment for 12 days. She was surprised and immediately came to Ched's room with me. Fortunately, Ched was lucid at that time and spoke with the dietician. He seemed happy to be able to communicate with her for a little while and when she suggested that she would send him some nutritional milk shakes like Ensure, he smiled and said, "Okay." Then he slipped back into his delirium once again, softly petting the animals that he saw lying in bed with him. I let him sip the Ensure whenever he was able which was not very often. He was getting weaker and weaker.

This Isn't Rocket Science

Ched was going to be sent to a nursing home to recuperate from his abdominal surgery, after 16 days in the hospital, still hallucinating, still not eating except for a few sips of Ensure, and still having episodes of severe anxiety. The nurses had to tie his arms and legs to the bed to restrain him. This was not the Ched that I knew. Something was very, very wrong… no one can tell me what was wrong. The neurologist still had not called me or come to check on Ched's condition!

I can't begin to tell you how frustrated I was. Retreating into my own thoughts, I silently screamed, thinking that someone could hear it, but no one seemed to notice. This whole ordeal was so upsetting to me. Hours passed into days with long nights of lost sleep. I was at the hospital 12 hours a day, 7 days a week for 16 days watching my beloved husband suffer and no one was able to tell me what was wrong with him. It doesn't take a rocket scientist to figure out that Ched was perfectly lucid the morning he went to the ER but two hours later after he was injected with a drug he never had before, his brain was fried! Was he given too much of the drug? Did he have a severe reaction to it? No doctor was willing to comment on that or explain what was happening to my husband.

Without a diagnosis from the medical doctors and their unwillingness to speak on behalf of the neurologist who never came to observe Ched, I was left to believe that the anti-seizure drug that the neurologist injected into Ched's vein in the ICU resulted in Ched's cognitive abilities being impaired so suddenly and to the extent that he was never the same again. But I admit, I am not a physician; this is just a wife's *opinion*, someone who was so frustrated by the lack of a diagnosis. I am sure all the doctors that I dealt with must have thought I was a nuisance to them because I wouldn't tolerate the brush-off I kept getting. I kept asking the questions; I kept insisting they rule out an overdose of the anti-seizure drug he was given. No answers to my questions, no workup on overdose because that wasn't their job, it was the neurologist's job, so around and around we went.

By this time, stress became the victor. I was becoming overloaded with anxiety so that my own cognitive abilities were becoming impaired. I was losing track of what the doctors were saying to me and I was becoming confused. My sons were becoming impatient with me. They were hearing one thing from the doctors and nurses while, it seemed, I was hearing something different. We were becoming at odds with one another and becoming very frustrated with everyone involved with Ched's care. We were desperate for someone to help us, but there was no one. In retrospect, I regret that I didn't know how to secure an advocate for me and for my sons. We were too close to this situation to think straight. We had no family other than ourselves and we didn't know who to contact in the hospital to help us. We were alone and we felt helpless.

After 16 post-op days in the hospital, Ched's condition had not improved at all. He was still hallucinating most of the time and sleeping a lot. There were times when suddenly he was lucid and for a few minutes he was the husband I knew again. He was able to remind me to pay the electric bill or some other bill that was due but then he would become confused and think that he already paid the bill. Those moments were encouraging for me. I thought perhaps he was coming out of that delirium and he would be on the road to recovery. But shortly afterwards, he went back to the world I could not see but could only perceive by the hallucinations he was experiencing. A psychiatrist was called in several times to evaluate him during his lucid moments and it was her opinion that Ched did not suffer from any psychiatric condition.

Hope Shattered

The attending physician came to speak to me one day and told me that they couldn't do anything more for Ched and they were going to send him to a nursing home to recover from his abdominal surgery just for a few weeks. When the doctor told me that, I became suspicious.

"Are you planning on discharging my husband to a nursing home because you don't know how to treat him any longer and you just want to be rid of him?" I asked the doctor.

"No, no." he said. We can't do anything more for him here, and we can't discharge him to go home with you. He is too weak; he can't walk. You won't be able to take care of him at home. Once he is at the nursing home, they will give him physical therapy, speech therapy, and all the necessary treatments to make him stronger so he would be able to go home again. It would only be for a few weeks." the doctor told me.

My mind raced. *A nursing home? That was someplace where people go to live out their lives and ultimately die there. I don't like what this doctor is telling me.* Then the discharge attending physician told me the words I wanted so desperately to hear.

"Once you get to the nursing home," he said, "the neurologist has sent orders to the physician on staff at the nursing home to begin weaning Ched off the anti-seizure drug."

I wanted to make sure I heard the doctor correctly so I repeated what he said and asked if he was certain the neurologist was sending the order to begin weaning Ched off that anti-seizure drug. He replied that this was correct. I was so relieved and happy at that point because I felt that once he was off that anti-seizure medication, his cognitive abilities would return. He wouldn't have to spend the rest of his life in a nursing home!

A transport service drove us to the nursing home and once we arrived, I immediately asked about the order sent from the neurologist to begin weaning Ched off the drug. I was told that no such order had been sent so I asked them to please check with the neurologist because I was given specific information from the attending physician in the hospital that the neurologist was sending the order to the nursing home. The head nurse checked on this and she was told that the hospital didn't send the order and Ched was to continue on the anti-seizure drug at the same strength he was on in the hospital.

I was livid! I called the neurologist's office and explained the situation.

"Has your husband ever been to our office before?" the nurse asked.

"No," I said. "Well, I'm sorry, we don't consider him to be our patient then." she said.

"What? You have got to be joking!" I said. "My husband was a patient of yours for 16 days in the hospital and the neurologist prescribed an anti-seizure medication for him which I would like to be discontinued. I am only asking that the doctor send an order to the physician at the nursing home to begin weaning him off the drug."

"I'm sorry, but unless he comes physically to our office, there is nothing we can do," she said impatiently.

I hastily replied, "My husband is immobile, I can't get him into a car to drive him to your office. I have to get an ambulance service to drive him and it will cost me $1,500.00 because my insurance won't pay to drive patients to doctors' visits."

Once again, she told me that unless he physically comes to the office, they don't consider him to be their patient.

I was stunned! Now what do we do? The doctor at the nursing home refused to wean Ched off the anti-seizure drug stating that they can only administer or discontinue drugs that came with the hospital's orders at the time of discharge. I pleaded and pleaded to no avail.

Note: A few months after Ched died, my insurance company notified all its clients that the neurologist at the hospital had ended his practice and went to a different state to set up another practice.

What Happened to Our Buddy?

While Ched was at the nursing home, an ambulance transport drove him to his dialysis treatments three days a week and brought him back when he was finished. The staff at the dialysis center couldn't believe their eyes when they saw Ched. He didn't recognize anyone; he was confused; he didn't want anyone to stick that large dialysis needle into his arm and he became very agitated even though the nurses tried to subdue him and explain what was happening. He sat in the chair with his head to his chest for the five hours of the dialysis treatment, sometimes screaming to be taken off, but of course, he had to remain for his treatment.

Ched was always a great story-teller and he was the nurses' favorite dialysis patient. He was a charmer and they loved to talk with him and laugh at his stories, but now, this man was no longer the Ched they knew. "What happened to him?" they would ask me. I told them what happened and they were shocked.

Ched continued to be transported to his kidney dialysis treatments from the nursing home with no improvement in his cognitive abilities. The dialysis nurses had a very hard time treating him because he became very anxious and he couldn't understand what they were doing to him. Because the dialysis staff could not reveal personal information about any of their patients, I was sure the other patients wondered what happened to their buddy, that nice guy who made everyone laugh and took away a lot of the tension during treatments.

Ched was almost like a zombie at times, not knowing who

these people were and what they were doing to him. When you spend so much time with these beautiful dialysis patients, they become like family. When you think of it, you see them more frequently than some of your own family - 15 hours a week, every week, month after month, year after year. So I made it a point to answer some of the patients who asked me a direct question about Ched's condition so they could understand.

There is great empathy between dialysis patients and their families who bring them for treatment. One day one patient doesn't come for treatment anymore and you know they died. You feel the loss. You even attend their funerals. You care about their families.

I remember one day Ched and I were talking about a dialysis patient who was expected to die within the next few days. I was very distraught because we came to love this patient and his wife. For several years that Ched was receiving his dialysis treatments, I sat in the waiting room with the man's wife and other wives of patients for the five long hours of dialysis treatments that our husbands were receiving. It was very upsetting for me to witness this man's illness threatening his life every time we went to the dialysis center, knowing that he would not live much longer. I told Ched how I felt.

"Nancy, you have to get used to this because we are all slowly dying; dialysis just buys us time because there is no cure," Ched calmly told me.

Then one day, like a burglar in the night, death stole this brave man's life and gave him his final rest. I'm sure that when their buddy Ched came for dialysis in the condition he was in, the staff and families probably thought that Ched was going downhill rapidly and that he would die soon. I can only imagine what it might be like for those dialysis patients to see other patients deteriorate knowing that in due time, they too, would worsen and inevitably die. I never had the courage to ask Ched if he was afraid of dying. I didn't want to risk the answer I might receive. I just wanted him to live forever.

Being an Advocate

While at the nursing home, they began giving Ched physical therapy to strengthen his muscles. At this point he had lost the ability to walk. He was now wheelchair bound. They started speech therapy to help with his cognitive skills. Nothing was helping. At times he didn't even know what was being asked of him and he sat motionless, eyes glazed over when he was being asked to do something. My heart would break.

I was Ched's advocate, honoring that unspoken but powerful contract that connected us for so many years. I was determined that he was treated with the dignity he deserved so I made certain the nursing home staff had me to deal with when things went amiss. I became like a lioness at times wanting to protect my loved one. Strange how one's own personality can change in an instant when trying to right a wrong. There were times however, when the stress of all this became hard for me to cope with and my sons became their father's advocate, taking over the necessary communication with the nursing staff to see to it that Ched's needs were taken care of. I was so grateful that I had my sons to help me in that regard.

Ched would fall out of bed onto the hard tiled floor so I would complain to the staff about doing something to protect him from falling out of bed and possibly breaking a bone. Most hospital beds have side rails for at-risk patients like this. But I was told the nursing home didn't provide side rails because some patients get their heads stuck in the rails and they can suffocate. The best they could do was to lay a mat on the floor for when he fell out of bed.

"Okay then, get him a mat NOW!" I insisted, "Because he falls out of bed frequently." But it wasn't until two days later that they finally provided a mat on the floor for him to fall onto.

Dear God, I don't know if I am capable of doing the work I am being called to do. I don't know if I have the strength to endure this heartache at this point in my life. I don't know if I am capable of comforting Ched when I can't even comfort myself. I am troubled and frightened, and fearful of the future. I feel worn down by the sheer weight of all that I am going through. Help me to keep my head above water so I don't drown; please help me so I can help Ched!

Comforting Spirits

Most of the time Ched was hallucinating. One time he looked at me and said, "Nancy, we better leave now, they are going to close. We'll be stuck here and we don't want to be arrested if they find us here."

I asked him where we were and he said we were at the Veterinary School at Ohio State University. I knew that he believed we were there so I didn't want to tell him he was hallucinating and upset him. I simply allowed him to tell me what he was seeing so he could feel comfortable talking about it with me. Other times when he was hallucinating, it was my opinion that he was seeing spirits from the other side, but I was not yet ready to consider that my beloved husband was on his way "home," that final home of all homes. I was still thinking that he would be at the nursing home until he regained enough strength to come home to me again. I should have recognized these signs coming from the spirit world preparing him (and me) for Ched's death, but I wasn't ready yet to heed those signs.

He often told me he saw animals lying in bed with him, some of which were our dogs that had previously died. He would smile and raise his hand to pet them and talk to them. I too, smiled because I knew that Ched was being loved by those animals he loved so much. I felt comforted every time I saw Ched's hand raise to pet one of the animals lying next to him in his bed. For all that Ched was going through, at least he was being loved through his ordeal by the animal spirits who came to comfort him. I can only imagine how much love filled his heart when he was able to see and interact with the beloved pets that were once part of our family. To this day, thinking of that is **extremely comforting** to me.

One day Ched called me to the side of his bed and he said softly, "There's my grandmother."

I asked, "Where is she?"

He pointed his finger at the corner of the wall and said, "She's standing there. Look! She's smiling at me."

Of course, I couldn't see his grandmother but I knew she was there. I looked at Ched watching his grandmother and the look on his face was absolutely beautiful. His facial expression softened, his eyes were misty, his smile was so sweet, like a little boy who loved his grandmother so much. I knew I was receiving a wonderful gift at that moment, sharing his grandmother's beautiful spiritual presence with him. I wanted the moment to last forever, but it ended. I silently thanked his grandmother's spirit for coming to him. That was such a precious gift to me to have witnessed my husband's grandmother's precious spiritual presence to him.

The thought did cross my mind at that time that perhaps his grandmother's spirit was a sign after all that Ched would die. I am very familiar with the literature filled with documented studies of bedside visits from deceased loved ones who come to aid the dying to help them cross over to the other side. But I didn't want to think that was going to happen soon, *no, no, not soon, please God, not soon!*

Beginning to Hope

I was still trying to figure out how to get that anti-seizure drug removed from Ched's system. After doing some investigative work, I learned that Ched's former neurologist was now practicing near the nursing home and she was accepting the insurance coverage we had for Ched. I immediately called her office and asked her to see Ched. She agreed. An ambulance service transported him to her office. When she saw Ched, she tried to remain expressionless, but I could see through that. She was shocked. Ched had been her patient for many years and she knew him well. When she no longer accepted the insurance Ched had, we had to find another neurologist to take over his care but this situation arose before we could do that. She asked a lot of questions and all I could do was tell her what happened.

I got the impression that doctors won't comment on other doctors' treatment even if they feel it was negligent. She would not comment on the treatment Ched received or didn't receive from the hospital neurologist. She did however, agree to wean him off the anti-seizure drug that the hospital neurologist prescribed by sending an order to the nursing home physician. I was elated! Finally! Finally! Finally! At last I was beginning to have hope that my husband would respond and eventually be able to come home to me but I was very wrong.

We saw Ched's former neurologist on a Friday afternoon. Monday morning the ambulance service drove him for his scheduled dialysis appointment. I stayed at home to rest awhile. Since December 29th, I had remained at Ched's beside for long hours, exhausted, and with very little sleep. I needed to wash Ched's clothes to take back to the nursing home after dialysis. I still had to perform household chores, pay bills, etc. his little break would be good for me. My sons saw how devoted I was to Ched and they helped me immensely by taking turns to stay with Ched when I was too exhausted. Someone was with him most of the time.

Back to the Hospital Again

Monday morning, I received a phone call from the head nurse at the dialysis center. "Nancy, Ched had a severe anxiety attack while on the dialysis machine. We could not restrain him and we had to call the squad to take him to the hospital," she said. I immediately stopped everything I was doing and drove to the hospital.

"What's wrong?" I asked the ER physician.

"I see by his history that he was in our hospital three weeks ago," the doctor said. "We are going to admit him and try and figure out what is wrong."

Oh no, here we go again. But perhaps this time someone can figure out what is wrong with Ched. I was beginning to have some hope again.

All the tests they performed were inconclusive and left the doctors still uncertain of a diagnosis. There were a number of doctors who came to evaluate Ched's condition and not one could tell me what was wrong. I was so sick of all this. I desperately wanted a diagnosis. I was so sick of sitting in a chair all day waiting for some sign of improvement. I was so sick of being told by a nurse that Ched was being weaned off the anti-seizure medication and he was not. Silently I cried tears of anguish, frustration and, most of all, fear of the unknown.

Gazing out of the window in Ched's room, I became aware of the blue sky, the bright sunshine and an occasional white cloud passing by. What a contrast from the dimly-lit hospital room and my own bleak thoughts that grasped my mind as I sat in that chair waiting for someone to come in the room with some good news. The waiting seemed endless.

One day a doctor came into the room and told me he was the partner of the neurologist who had prescribed that anti-seizure drug during Ched's stay in ICU weeks earlier. This neurologist had been asked to check on Ched. At last! A neurologist connected to that first one was here to follow up on Ched!

I wondered why the neurologist who administered the anti-seizure drug to Ched in ICU weeks earlier wasn't the physician who came to evaluate Ched this time? It was his partner instead. It seemed strange to me, but I gave him the benefit of the doubt. Perhaps he was too busy, or perhaps he didn't want to deal with me. I was just so thankful that a neurologist – any neurologist-was on Ched's case this time. Perhaps now, we would learn what was wrong with Ched's brain.

The neurologist did a brief exam and couldn't tell me much. Ched wasn't able to perform the simple neurological tests that were being asked of him. I asked if the anti-seizure drug that his partner prescribed for him could be the culprit, but he didn't think it was. He thought maybe it was a virus that attacked the brain but the only way to find out was to do a spinal tap. I knew Ched could not tolerate this exam in the condition he was in and the doctor agreed. So basically, there was no way to diagnose his condition from what the neurologist told me.

In Ched's condition, he couldn't tolerate an MRI or any other test that required him to be quiet and be still. I told the neurologist that he was being weaned off the anti-seizure drug as directed by his former neurologist and he agreed to continue with that protocol while Ched was in the hospital. The process of weaning him off that drug would take months, but at least we were starting, and I was hopeful.

After about two weeks in the hospital, Ched was still not eating much. He was very weak by now. The hospital bed rails were in the up position so that Ched would not fall out of bed. I was grateful for this precaution in lieu of a mat on the floor like the nursing home had for him. Every doctor that came to see him still could not figure out what was wrong with him or how to treat him. He simply took up bed space and we waited and waited for some change, but nothing changed.

A Right to Die

I knew in my heart that Ched did not want to live this way. For many years we had discussed end of life issues and we both agreed that should we ever be in a condition where the quality of life was no longer there for us, we would choose to die with dignity instead of living like a vegetable just living to exist. In Ched's case, being a dialysis patient, he had the right to discontinue dialysis treatments with the understanding that in doing so, he would die. This is what Ched wanted to do in the event that his quality of life was no longer good.

He always told me, "I would rather die than simply exist in a state where I couldn't enjoy life anymore."

I understood his wishes. He lived on his own terms. He was happy with the life he had lived, happy with the woman who was at his side for over fifty years, happy with his two sons that made him so proud. If he wanted to die on his own terms, I would not try to stop him. I loved him enough to honor his wishes and release him.

Where did this strength come from? I wondered. Is it possible that the inner resources that reside in my heart are guiding me in making this decision? This decision was clearly written in a language that my heart understood and helped me to transcend the challenge that confronted me. I was putting Ched's needs above my own. That remarkable inner resource was unconditional love, and it showed me the power and depth of my love for Ched.

Stop Dialysis Treatments!

I remember that morning very well. I woke up and knew that this was the day when I would tell his doctor to discontinue Ched's dialysis treatments. I was Ched's advocate and had legal power of attorney in all his health care decisions. It was time for me to love Ched so much that I was willing to let him go.

Oh God, help me to do this for him. Oh God, give me the strength. I can't live without Ched. My God, help me, help me! I cried until I couldn't cry any longer. This was going to be the day.

I arrived at the hospital on a cold and chilly February morning, and entered the hospital through the maternity door entrance. It was the entrance closest to me and I wanted to get inside the building quickly because I was cold. I noticed that a young woman was being pushed in a wheelchair by her husband and she was carrying her newborn baby to take home with them. Red and yellow colored balloons were tied to the handles of the wheelchair and some baskets of flowers were at her feet. I smiled at them and they acknowledged my smile.

My mind raced with a mixture of joy and pain. This young couple were beginning a new life together with their new-born baby and they were so happy. There would be so many wonderful experiences they would have to look forward to. As I walked past them, memories of my own life with Ched and our new-born sons flashed swiftly through my mind.

Looking back on so many years that had passed, I could still recall the sense of wonder that Ched and I both felt when we held our sons in our arms. Our love created those miracles and we both understood that it was imperative that we would be good parents, and we were.

A hospital is a place where there is life and death, joy and sorrow, and for those few moments when I passed those new parents, I felt happy. Then quickly I realized why I was walking through the corridors toward Ched's room. This was the day when the decision about life and death was going to be made. My throat tightened as I thought that he would never again see the sunshine or the rain, our home, or the smell of a home cooked meal. He would never see his friends, his sister or his brothers again, or help our sons with any problems they might have. He would never continue to share his life with me again.

Oh God, please be with me and give me the courage and strength to follow through with the decision to end his dialysis treatments so he can die in peace, I silently cried out.

God heard my cries. Somewhere deep inside of me, as I found the strength to keep walking toward his hospital room, an inner voice kept reminding me that this is what Ched wanted. He did not want to live this way. It was time to set him free from this agonizing existence.

The doctor was outside of Ched's room reviewing his chart when I approached. I was just ready to tell him about the decision I made to discontinue Ched's dialysis treatments but I didn't have that opportunity. Ched did not know I was outside of his hospital room or that the doctor was checking his chart. No words had been spoken yet to alert Ched to our presence.

Suddenly, Ched called out, "No more dialysis! No more!"

I couldn't believe what I just heard. Surprised, the doctor and I looked at each other and we immediately went into Ched's room. The doctor and I stood close to Ched.

Once again, Ched shouted, "No more dialysis!"

I asked if he understood what that meant and he said, "Yes, I will die within one to two weeks."

I replied, "Yes, Ched, that is correct, you will die in one to two weeks. Is that what you want?"

He said firmly, "YES!"

While stroking his head, I told him that I would honor his wishes. He looked into my loving eyes and smiled, and I noticed that his entire body relaxed as if the weight of the world had just been lifted from his shoulders. He fell asleep immediately and at peace.

I looked at the doctor, relieved that Ched was the one who was able to convey his own wishes about how and when he wanted to die. It was a gift he was able to give to me so I wouldn't have the burden on my own already weakened shoulders. He was still the strong rock I had always relied on for all our most important decisions in life, this of course, being *the* most important one.

Palliative Care

I turned to the doctor who stood beside me and I asked him, "What do we do now?"

He said, "I witnessed Ched's decision to terminate further dialysis treatments. I am going to speak to the director of the palliative care unit and we will move him to that unit for the duration of his care. He will continue to be treated as he has been, nothing will change. We will take good care of him until nature ends his life."

Lost in my thoughts, I didn't want to admit to myself the magnitude, intensity, or tenacity of my pain. I was tempted to seal it over with my courage, knowing that it was Ched's decision to die. Like golden threads, Ched had always been woven into the tapestry of my life and in the lives of our two sons. I didn't want to think of our lives without him. No, I must only focus upon his hospital care at this time, making sure the doctors and nurses would do their part in making him comfortable during his final days on earth. I would live one day at a time, moment to moment, allowing my spirit to take care of me while I watched

Ched's spirit slowly ebb away. That was my plan, a plan that allowed me to face the greatest ordeal of my life.

Once he was moved to the palliative care unit, the type of medical and supportive efforts employed to care for a patient when the patient is considered no longer responsive to curative treatments, was set in place. The nurses took good care of Ched. They explained what was happening to his physical body so that I wouldn't become suddenly alarmed. I stayed at his bedside all day while my sons took turns after work to be with him at night. There were times when he awoke and was lucid. We would talk for brief moments before he fell asleep again. Since he wasn't eating any hospital food, I asked him if he was hungry; I could bring something from home for him. His eyes opened wide; he smiled and said "Yes, I would like something from home."

The next morning I tried to figure out what to take him. The refrigerator was nearly empty, I hadn't gone to the grocery store in months because I was home only to sleep and I would grab a small bite to eat in the hospital cafeteria or at the vending machine at the nursing home. I finally decided upon some cold shrimp that I defrosted to bring to the hospital for Ched. When I pulled out the container with the shrimp and cocktail sauce and told him what it was, he was so happy. I fed it to him and he enjoyed it so much. The nurse happened to come in at that time and saw how Ched was eating the shrimp I was giving him.

"Look," she said, "He's eating it just like a little bird, stretching out to be fed."

We all laughed. Ched was only able to tolerate eating about 4 shrimp and no more. That was the last time he ate again. That memory comforts me with that small act of love I was able to do for him.

I brought a digital tape recorder with me when I went to visit Ched. I waited for those precious moments when he was lucid and he could speak to me. I wanted to record his voice so I would always be able to hear it once it was silenced forever. I would never forget how it sounded. I am so glad I did that. One time when he was able to speak I asked him if he was afraid and he said, "No, I don't think so," and then he fell asleep suddenly.

His last mumbled words to me were, "I love you."

From the time he was moved to palliative care, the doctor continued to come in and assess his condition, and give him medicines that that would help him to remain comfortable. As the days went on, the doctor explained that his organs would slowly shut down as the toxins in his body would build up. Dialysis, of course, removed the build-up of toxins in the body; but now the body couldn't remove them and some would come out through the pores of his body. I should expect to smell it. As a result, Ched would experience a lot of itching.

Gradually, he would lose the ability to swallow and secretions would build up in his throat which the nurses would have to remove. I believe that was the worst part of witnessing Ched's dying process. Those secretions would build up and with that, his epiglottis would rattle with every breath he took. Those death rattles were very hard to listen to. It sounded as if he were struggling for air to breathe, but fortunately he was not awake to know he was experiencing that. He slept more and more and, eventually, he entered into a coma. In that state, he would die peacefully.

He had developed C-diff, a highly communicable colitis condition, and I was warned not to touch him without having protective measures in place, gloves, a mask, and a gown. I wanted so much to be able to crawl into the bed with him and hold him so close to my body, feeling his breath upon mine as I kissed him so tenderly, just to hold him, but I wasn't allowed to do this because I would place myself at great risk for developing C-diff.

Instead, I held him in my heart, in deep silence and stillness, talking to him and telling him how much I loved him. Silent words of deep-seated gratitude for the man who became my husband and father to our wonderful sons felt as if those words were part of love's rainbow. Each word I spoke in the silence of my heart entered into a world of heavenly light that extended into the gates of heaven to carry Ched's ebbing spirit to the next phase of his eternal existence. Those words in my heart in essence became a hotline to my unconscious husband's soul and to God's ear. I felt comforted in believing that they both heard my silent words, for the language of love knows no boundaries. The spirit of love that connected us could never be broken.

I sat by his bedside from early morning until evening's voice whispered to me that it was time to drive home and get some much needed rest. But how could I sleep? There were incessant thoughts robbing me of the sleep I yearned for. *This must be a nightmare; no, this is reality. Soon Ched will die. How will I go on?* Thoughts were endless. My body ached for peace. Sleep descended upon me at last. Another morning arrived, another drive to the hospital, another hard chair to sit on while I watch my beloved slowly die.

One evening while my son Randy and I were leaving the hospital for the evening, Randy suddenly said, "I just realized I will never be able to ask dad how to do or fix things anymore. Dad was so smart. What a shame that his wisdom and knowledge will be lost to us forever."

Randy's eyes became misty as he spoke, his voice strained with the understanding that his dad was dying and we would never be able to rely on Ched for his guidance again.

Like a sharp razor cutting into my own mind, Randy's words suddenly brought me to the same realization. It became apparent to me that Randy was correct; we wouldn't be able to ask Ched how to do so many things we were unsure of doing ourselves. His gift to us would come to a screeching halt and we would have to navigate on our own once he left us. My thoughts became almost palpable. *It isn't fair! He is leaving us too soon! We still need him!*

March 9, 2011

So many memories were flooding through my mind as I watched my precious husband slowly die. Those memories of Ched's love for our family reminded me of his character and his values in life. I felt so honored to have shared my life with this wonderful human being. But now as his spirit was slowly ebbing away just as a point of light slowly disappears into nothingness, I wondered how I could live without him. How would his death affect Chris and Randy? There were no answers.

Ched was now sleeping most of the time, unable to speak. I was told he wouldn't wake up anymore, he was in the coma. At 2:00 am, March 9, 2011, the hospital called. I knew what the nurse was about to say.

"Your husband passed about 10 minutes ago." she said.

"I'll be right over," I replied.

Shock, disbelief, relief, those were the emotions I felt immediately after I hung up the phone. I had wanted desperately to be with him at the moment of his death. I did not want him to die alone. But I have learned that, most of the time, patients who die in the hospital wait until family members have gone home. It is as if they want to spare their loved ones the pain of seeing them die so they depart after the family leaves the hospital. I called my son to drive me to the hospital. It was a chilly, rainy evening and the half-hour drive to the hospital was rather subdued; we didn't talk much. I guess we were both lost in our own thoughts at the time.

A hospital chaplain accompanied us to Ched's room and stood by while we said our final goodbyes and then she offered a prayer. She explained the papers I needed to sign and explained that Ched's body would be removed to the hospital morgue to await being taken to the funeral home. I cried softly knowing this was the last time I would ever see Ched again. Desperately, I tried to imprint his face upon my memory so I would never forget it.

I wondered what my son Chris was thinking as I witnessed soft tears streaming down his face. His dad had always been an amazing father and friend to him, and now he was experiencing his own loss in his own way. My heart broke for Chris. When the chaplain began to motion to us that it was time to leave, Chris and I took our final gaze upon Ched's lifeless body and we left.

Where did this inner strength come from, I wondered? I am accepting Ched's death in some unexplainable way. The love of my life is gone and I am walking through the corridors of the hospital with my son as if I were just going home after my visit with Ched. *Why am I not falling down on my knees begging God to return my precious husband to me? Why am I not screaming? Why do I feel this inner peace instead?*

I guess the body has its own way of coping when tragedy occurs and every person experiences their reactions in different ways. Mine, I believe, was through the gracious blessing of God who was with me the entire time. I know that God's love for Ched and me was the glue that held us together for over fifty years, and now that Ched had left me behind to carry on, God would still see to it that I had the strength to go on without Ched. The peace that "passeth all understanding" is the peace I felt that evening when Ched was called home to be with God. But it didn't last long.

"The caterpillar dies so the butterfly could be born. And, yet, the caterpillar lives in the butterfly and they are but one. So, when I die, it will be that I have been transformed from the caterpillar of earth to the butterfly of the universe."

—John Harricharan

3

Roller Coaster Emotions

*"Grief is not a disorder, a disease or a sign of weakness. It is
an emotional, physical and spiritual necessity, the price you
pay for love. The only cure for grief is to grieve."*

—Earl Grollman

I was familiar with the five stages of grief that Elisabeth
Kubler-Ross, MD described. They are: denial, anger, bargain-
ing, depression, and acceptance. Elisabeth herself did not intend
these stages to be cut in stone or one size fits all. She stated in
her last book in 2004, *"They were never meant to help tuck messy
emotions into neat packages. They are responses to loss that many
people have, but **there is not a typical response to loss, as there is
no typical loss.** Our grieving is as individual as our lives."* This was
so important for me to understand so I didn't worry about what
I "should" be feeling or what stage I was supposed to be in. In
fact, I understood that I didn't have to go through each of these
five stages in order to heal the grief that I felt.

If I have learned anything at all from my own grief process,
it is this: anything one experiences during the grief process is
normal – including feeling like you are going crazy, feeling that
you will soon wake up from a bad dream, or that you have roller
coaster emotions that are full of ups and downs. It is not enough

to KNOW about grief from an intellectual perspective, but rather, one must FEEL it from the heart!

I vaguely remember that morning when I came home from the hospital after Ched died. I was in shock but I didn't realize it. I kept thinking this was a dream and I would wake up. But I also knew what the reality was. My soul-mate had just died and my life would never be the same again. I cried the entire day and night, sobbing so hard, my blood pressure rose. I knew I had to be careful about that so I tried to repress my feelings, but I couldn't. A dam had burst wide open and any attempt to stop the flood was like trying to stick a wad of gum in the dam, so I just let the tears flow until sleep gave me some reprieve and gave my wounded body rest.

I didn't have the energy to call anyone to let them know that Ched died except my two brothers in Pennsylvania, and Ched's two brothers in Virginia, and his sister who lived in Pennsylvania. While they all expressed their sympathy, they decided not to travel to Ohio because there would not be any funeral service, only cremation which was Ched's wishes. It would only be me and my two sons to struggle through this process by ourselves, each trying to comfort one another as best we could.

"The best way out is always through."

—Robert Frost

Oh God, how will I get through the ordeal of visiting the funeral home to make the arrangements for cremation? I cried. If only I could sleep through this nightmare so I didn't have to face the reality of what I had to do. If only someone else could do this for me. If only there was some other way to handle this ordeal. I wanted to feel like a baby again, cradled in the arms of my mother being protected and soothed from all this anguish. But I knew there was no other way. My grieving sons came with me and we put one foot in front of the other and we did it. We had no other option.

Days later, when Ched's obituary was published in the news-paper, people began phoning me to express their condolences. The first one to call me was my very dear friend, a psychologist. I was so happy to hear his voice, I cried. Someone cared about me and the anguish I must be going through! His compassionate voice was like a warm blanket that brought warmth to my shivering and shaking body. I was finally able to give a voice to my pain to someone who wanted to help me. But the words were few — the sobs spoke the words for me, but I knew my friend was there for me in the midst of my anguish and that was of tremendous comfort to me.

I expressed some of my feelings to him such as my disbelief. I couldn't believe what had happened. Of course I knew the reality of the situation, but I could not fathom that Ched wouldn't walk through the rooms of the house again or that I wouldn't hear his sweet laughter again. I wondered how I could go on without him, if I could go on, and why I should go on. I just wanted to be with Ched so much that my feelings were getting all mixed up.

My psychologist friend told me that I wasn't losing my mind, but that the mind was simply protecting me as a way of shutting out the harsh reality so I would begin to adjust to my loss. When events are so overwhelming the human body has a mechanism in place to protect us that way. After my friend and I talked, I silently thanked my spirit for protecting me this way and allowing me only to handle as much as I could and not more.

I have never before experienced such heart-wrenching, painfully raw emotions in my entire life. On a physical level, the pain would be a 10 on the pain scale. On an emotional level, the pain was off the charts. I am told that the number one most painful emotional crisis a human being can go through is the loss of a child, or the loss of a spouse. The longer a couple has been married and if it was a very happy marriage, the longer the grief process would take. That information was helpful for me to learn.

An Analogy of Grief

"The death of a beloved is an amputation."

—C.S. Lewis, *A Grief Observed*

Almost everyone who has a limb amputated will experience a phantom limb-the sinister sensation that one's limbs are still there. The nerve endings at the site of the amputation continues to send pain signals to the brain that make the brain think the limb is still there.

When Ched died, it felt as if a part of my core-self died. This amputation of a part of me was like phantom pain. No pain medication can fix it; it can only be tolerated until it fades. Like nerve endings attached to the very soul of my being, the pain resurfaced again like phantom pain, one day silent, the next, unbearable. I was left to find my way without my legs, to see without my eyes, and to feel without my heart.

An amputee begins the slow process of rehabilitation and begins to learn how to live without that missing limb. So it is with the loss of a loved one. At some point during the journey through grief, I will begin my own slow rehabilitation process of learning how to live again without that missing part of myself.

But I will have the faith that one day God will show me how to live again with new legs, new eyes, and a new heart that will enable me to fulfill the purpose for which I have been created.

> *"Grief is like the ocean; it comes on waves ebbing and flowing. Sometimes the water is calm, and sometimes it is overwhelming. All we can do is learn to swim."*
>
> —Vicki Harrison

Don't Rush the Process

In some ways, I still feel powerless after Ched's death; power-less to change the situation, powerless to control my emotions, powerless to control that which is beyond control. I can still fall apart at any given moment, whether I am outdoors gardening, watching TV, driving in my car, or walking up the driveway after getting the mail. A sudden surge of emotion overcomes me and I allow it to pour over me as if I am standing beneath a water-fall. I can gaze at Ched's photo and long for his touch, his hug, his laughter, having our morning coffee together as he joyfully counted the number of bird species that flew in that morning to the birdfeeder. I miss all those little daily events that would let me know how deeply we were both loved.

Allowing myself to FEEL those emotions is in some strange way, comforting. It allows me to get in touch with the deep-est part of myself, the self that was also part of Ched. For this reason, I will not rush the process of grief but rather, allow it to unfold naturally, according to my own timetable and no one else's. I will allow my feelings to ebb and flow throughout my life until as T.S. Eliot says, *"The end of our journey will be to arrive where we started and know the place for the first time."*

I will hold to the promise that others who have gone before me tell me that grief won't last forever, even though right at this moment, I think it will. I still have trouble knowing how to exit gracefully from the dark void I often feel. But I also understand that the dark void is also not a dead end. There are moments when there is a union of opposites – light and dark which serves to guide me on this incredible journey toward wholeness that I am working toward.

Eventually, I will be able to remember and honor Ched with-out feeling the unbearable pain I felt during the early stages of my grief. I will always miss my soul-mate, but I am grateful for having loved him so much, because as George Eliot once said,

"Only in the agony of parting do we look into the depths of love."

Nowhere in history will the same thoughts be going on in anyone's mind, soul and spirit. Grieving is unique to everyone going through it and it is important that we don't compare our reactions to another's, or one person's pain to another's. We all hurt when we face the death of a loved one. Pain is pain, no matter how it looks on the outside. We need to express our grief in a way that feels most real to us. For me, I could not control my tears. I missed Ched's physical presence with me so much that I would sob every single day, even to the present day. This helps to release the tension and sadness that wells up inside of me with no place to go except through the outpouring of my tears.

"There is a sacredness in tears. They are not the mark of weakness, but of power. They speak more eloquently than ten thousand tongues. They are the messengers of overwhelming grief, of deep contrition, and of unspeakable love."

—Washington Irving

I can't begin to tell you how many times while I have been talking on the telephone with a friend who says, "You sound GREAT!" There is an assumption that I am back to my old self again and I am over my grief. My reply is usually something like this, "That's because I am talking to you my friend, and I am happy to talk with you. I'm very happy you called."

But after I hang up the phone, I can burst out crying again because I know that I am not "great" as my friend assumes I am. For just a few minutes my spirit was lifted by a phone call from a dear friend. Yes, perhaps my voice did sound as if I was happy and back to my normal self, but I am not. I still miss Ched so much! I feel lost without him!

I want to talk to him about the home repairs we need to take care of. I want to ask him what he would like me to make for dinner. I want to walk with him in the garden and show him the flowers that had just bloomed, or just sit with him on the bench seat by the fish pond without having to say a single word while the warm sun washes over us. Oh, how I miss laughing with him every single day!

The hushed silence in the house is now surreal, broken only by the tick-tock of the clock on the wall and my cat's occasional meow to tell me he needs some attention. When the silence becomes too much, I play soft music in the background while I work. Alas, the journey through grief is a roller coaster ride of emotions, but that journey is always headed on a path toward the eventual healing of the wound that will slowly close up, leaving a healed scar. Grief will present me with the challenge to decide whether or not to accept my destiny, those first steps of a journey calling me to move through this darkness to discover the infinite power of the light.

"The only courage that matters is the kind that gets you from one moment to the next."

—Mignon McLaughlin

4

COPING WITH GRIEF

"If you are going through hell, just keep going."

—Winston Churchill

Sharing one's grief with others makes the burden of grief easier to bear. However, in our society, we are not comfortable with the subject of death. Our family and friends have unrealistic expectations of our grief process and how long it should take. Because they are well-meaning and love us, they are uncomfortable with our grief and that usually means they want us to hurry and get over it as soon as possible.

I may not be able to live up to others' expectations of me. I may not be ready to join the land of the living and prefer instead, to be alone with my sadness. This is a normal part of the grief process and I won't feel pressured to be anything other than who I am capable of being at any given time. People are moving on with their lives, but they don't realize that I have been stopped abruptly in my tracks and I can't move forward yet. It may take months, even years before I can fully heal from my heartbreak.

"They say time heals all wounds, but that presumes the source of the grief is finite.

—Cassandra Clare, *Clockwork Prince*

Shocking Comments

For most people, the idea of reaching out to a grief-stricken person is awkward. They simply don't know what to say, being fearful of saying the wrong thing. So they avoid saying anything.

"When a person is born we rejoice, and when they're married we jubilate, but when they die we try to pretend that nothing has happened."

—Margaret Mead

I remember when this happened to me. Some of my dearest friends avoided calling me or didn't say anything when I was with them. This made me ask myself, *Do they not know, or do they just not care?* As a result, I felt uncared for. It was a time when I needed someone to express their concern and compassion, a gift that would have made a big difference in lightening my load at that time. I was however, aware that I needed to forgive them and I found it helpful to say, *They just don't get it.*

One evening when I came home exhausted from the hospital where Ched lay dying, the phone rang. It was a good friend who cared about me and wanted to know how I was doing. I said, "I don't know what I will do without Ched."

Immediately, my friend said, "Look, I'm going to give you some tough love right now so you don't make yourself a martyr out of this."

I couldn't believe what I just heard. I was so shocked that I cannot remember what he said for the next ten minutes that he spoke. Instead of providing comfort when I expressed how lost I would feel without Ched, he lectured me about how I "should" feel.

Two months after Ched died, this same friend emailed me and told me it was time for me to be happy again. Happy again? Did he think I could just stop grieving and move on with my life so soon after Ched died? How does anyone know when it is time for another person to stop grieving? The only person who knows when it is time to stop grieving is the one who is grieving.

Due to all the mixed up emotions that grieving presented for me, I was very sensitive to comments from people who wanted to "fix me" by getting me over my grief quickly. Those comments were not supporting me; they were painful for me to hear. Yet, I knew they loved and cared for me; they just didn't fully understand how to provide meaningful support for me during this difficult time.

Let's Not Talk About This

Several times some of my friends would often ask me how I was doing but were not prepared to listen to what I had to say. For example, I responded to one friend with, "Well, I'm not doing very well at this time" and felt tears welling up in my eyes.

She immediately apologized for bringing it up, saying, "I can see this is making you sad. Let's change the subject."

Here was an opportunity for her to be a real friend and actually listen to me or comfort me with a simple hug; to empathize with my feelings. I would have considered that a virtue instead of a problem. But my grief was uncomfortable for her and she didn't want to get involved. She had encouraged me to talk and I wanted to talk, but she didn't want to listen.

"Where grief is fresh, any attempt to divert it only irritates."

—Samuel Johnson

Half of Me Is Missing

Others judged my grief with teachings that made no sense to me. To their way of thinking, when a person grieves, it means that something is wrong with our understanding of life and our relationships with one another. I was told that one of the reasons I was experiencing feelings of grief, was because I believed I needed another person, specifically Ched, to make me feel whole and complete. I was told that people do not need other people to make them feel whole because we are whole to begin with. I was told that I am *choosing* to experience suffering, and I could also *choose not* to suffer as well.

So I was instructed to change my understanding of my need to feel *connected* to Ched so that I wouldn't miss him because that was the cause of my pain and suffering. Once I would *choose* to do that, I wouldn't miss Ched anymore. Are you kidding? I will miss Ched until the day I die and I didn't need to be told that this was somehow wrong.

Well, it was indeed true that it seemed like a part of me had died with Ched and I was no longer the whole person I had been before. That was my honest feeling and I didn't need to be told that this was somehow wrong thinking. Who can judge if a feeling is right or wrong? At the time, I felt like a huge chunk of my heart had been ripped out and that part of my spirit-self accompanied Ched's spirit on his journey "home."

During intense periods of grief it really did seem like the part of me that was so connected to and left with Ched would be missing forever, never to return again. It would have been helpful to me to have had my friends simply listen to me without making any judgments about my feelings and the way I needed to grieve. They didn't need to feel any responsibility in lecturing me and judging me so that I would no longer grieve. I'm grieving as fast as I can, but unfortunately, it isn't fast enough for some well-meaning and loving people.

"Without you in my arms, I feel an emptiness in my soul. I find myself searching the crowds for your face. I know it's an impossibility, but I cannot help myself."

—Nicholas Sparks, Message in a Bottle

Friends' Suggestions

Some of my friends wanted me to stop missing Ched so much and told me so. I am entitled to my own feelings, whatever they are. I will make no apologies for missing my beloved husband so much. He was my world, my best friend, my lover, my soul-mate, that soft place I could land on when I needed to be comforted. I think there would be something wrong with me if I **didn't miss him so much!**

Someone gave me a solution to end my grief. "Stop thinking of Ched so much. When you start to feel sad, change your thoughts to happy thoughts and then you will feel better."

I didn't want to repress my feelings; I wanted to feel them and actively deal with them. Trying to ignore the pain or keep it from surfacing would only make it worse in the long run. I had enough sense not to take that advice coming from my well-meaning friends.

Another suggestion someone made was, "Put away all of Ched's photos so you aren't being reminded of him."

Actually, one of the first things I did after Ched died was gather as many photos as possible and place them in every room so I could always see him. I would have been very content to wallpaper all the walls in my house with his photos; they brought me such comfort. Even now, in looking at and talking to his photo, I feel the silence of our home awaken to a human voice again, and visually, I am comforted when I look at his photos.

One of the comments I hated to hear was, "I know how you feel."

I wanted to say, "No, you don't know how I feel. It's impossible to feel someone else's feelings because you can only feel your own feelings. You have no clue how I feel!"

One woman I know told me, "I know exactly how you feel. My dog died and I felt awful."

Seriously, comparing the death of a dog to the death of a spouse, or a child, or any other human being who had been intensely loved? Granted, the death of a beloved pet is an agonizing experience to go through. I had so many beloved pets who died and each one was heartbreaking to lose. But please don't say something like that to a grieving person whose loved one has died!

Another comment that I didn't appreciate was, "You are strong Nancy, you will be fine."

No, I wasn't strong! I felt weak, vulnerable, and unsure of what my future held for me without Ched. He was my rock, the one I depended upon. Now that rock had shattered into a million tiny particles of sand with no way to ever put my rock back together again.

We have a large bookcase filled with many books. For Christmas one year Ched bought me some gorgeous natural stone bookends for that bookcase. We used to tell one another that we were similar to those bookends displayed in the bookcase. He held me up and I held him up, like bookends. We knew that when one of us was gone, the center structure would fall down just as the books would fall without the support of both bookends.

Well, that is exactly what happened when he died. Now I have the sole responsibility of holding myself upright without his stabilizing force. Some days I struggle to hold myself up; I waver and fall down. I find it is a daily struggle for me, especially when

I see those beautiful stone bookends on the shelf holding the books together like Ched and I used to do for one another. My rock is gone now. I must accept that. How will I ever do that?

Some of my friends used to tell me, "Everything will be alright, Nancy, don't worry."Everything was NOT alright! My world came crashing down right before my eyes as if I were being swallowed up by an earthquake and fell into a deep, dark crevice. Emotionally I was bleeding profusely and struggling to get out of that crevice while people were passing by, not realizing I was injured. My mind raced, *Will anyone help me or will they keep passing by without even trying?*

I don't expect anyone to repair my injured wounds because no one can! I just need a steady, compassionate hand to help me climb out from beneath the rubble and navigate upward toward the light. Once that is done, then perhaps I can believe that everything will be alright; but right now I am not alright! Please don't demean my feelings! Lend me a compassionate hand to help me rise again, that's all!

As human beings, we were created to need one another. Our God-given gift of human compassion enables us to show one another that we really do care even when tempted to say or do nothing. I deeply appreciated the hands of compassion offered to me from my friends even if it was just a hug with no words being said. A silent hug placed a bandage of love on my bruised and bleeding heart and it helped me.

"When your fear touches someone's pain, it becomes pity. When your love touches someone's pain, it becomes compassion."

—Stephen Levine

Call Me

Many of my friends said, "If I can do anything, call me."

That is a common expression, but I didn't feel like picking up the phone and asking someone to please bring me a casserole for dinner because I wasn't eating well. That laid the burden on me to ask for help when I couldn't think straight. I would have preferred that they bring me that casserole, or offer to go to the grocery store to pick up a few things that I might have needed. I would have appreciated phone calls from friends who would allow me to talk or cry without trying to change the subject because it was uncomfortable for them.

Nutrition is Important

I remember going to the grocery store for the first time several weeks following Ched's death. I had not been eating well. I wasn't preparing any meals because I didn't have the energy or the desire. No one brought casseroles to the house or thought to consider that I might not be getting adequate nutrition. My refrigerator was pretty empty for months, so I had to force myself to go to the grocery store. I felt lost! Aimlessly, I walked up and down the aisles not knowing what to put in my shopping cart.

Every time I went grocery shopping in the past, I was always thinking of Ched's needs. Being on dialysis, he couldn't have certain foods; I had to read all labels and watch for phosphorus and potassium levels in foods. I was always planning meals around what he was able to eat and enjoy. But now, I didn't have to think of his needs any more, I could just think about me. It was nearly impossible for me to do this. My brain felt frozen; I couldn't think. After two hours and feeling mentally exhausted from trying to figure out what I would like to eat, I had one carton of blackberries, one container of yogurt and one dozen eggs in my cart. I came home with only those items.

I was still not eating well and about two months after Ched died, my dear friend who is a nurse called and said she was bringing me some dinner. She brought spaghetti, salad, rolls, and a bottle of wine. We sat down and shared the meal together. That was my first real meal since Ched died, but more than that, she didn't wait for me to call her and ask her to do anything for me, like most people wanted me to do. She just did it. I will NEVER forget what her **love in action** meant to me that day.

That dear friend also placed some of Ched's ashes inside a specially made heart-shaped necklace that I bought that has a tiny urn inside it to place the ashes of a loved one. After gently and carefully putting some of Ched's ashes in the urn, she then super-glued the necklace parts together. I will never forget this simple act of kindness! I wear that necklace all the time.

So often, my friends tried to be a grief experts when they were not. They tried to change what I was saying or thinking so I would become more cheerful. I didn't want my friends to push me through the grief process with advice, solutions, or cures they thought would help. They were trying to "fix" me and I wasn't ready for that.

What happened as a result of that was that I began to hide my feelings to avoid those quick, unpleasant comments. That took me and the other person off the hook from further talk about my feelings, but the truth is, that I am not fine. I miss my husband every single day! Expressing these feelings would be healthier than hiding them, but others didn't want to hear about my grief after a while. I believe that is one of the reasons grief lasts as long as it does; eventually the grieving person grows silent and internalizes the pain without expression.

"A true friend is someone who sees the pain in your eyes while everyone else believes the smile on your face.

—Author unknown

A Family Hobby

Our very first car after Ched and I got married was a British Austin Healey sports car and we have had one ever since. Our entire family became very involved in the local Austin Healey and Triumph sports car clubs, attending meetings, going on car cruises and entering competitions. Ched won numerous awards for the vintage 1966 Austin Healey 3000 that he and my son restored. Ched was president of the Mid-Ohio Austin Healey Club for several years and our entire family loved sharing this wonderful hobby together.

Our sons grew up learning how to repair and restore these beautiful cars from their dad and even mom got involved. Her specialty was sitting in the driver's seat with a book in hand bleeding the brakes while Ched or one of the boys worked on them. Talk around the dinner table was usually about the Austin Healey events we were going to go to or about a diagnostic problem the guys were facing that a good analytical discussion would usually resolve. This hobby bonded all of us together so beautifully.

Eventually, our sons each bought several Austin Healeys and participated in all the car events along with Ched and me. The car cruises with the members of the Austin Healey and Triumph car clubs were so enjoyable. We would meet someplace and then drive for several hours through the countryside, convertible tops down, sports cars following one another, the breeze blowing through our hair, the warm sun in our faces – a slice of Heaven!

But after Ched died, a strange thing happened to me. I couldn't bear to attend a meeting with members of the car clubs anymore. I didn't want to drive on the cruises. Ched wasn't with me and it was a painful reminder to be around those friends for that reason. Seven months after he died, I did go to a pond party hosted by our Austin Healey friends who lived on a beautiful, large country estate. Ched and I had attended these parties for many years. Everyone would sit on hay bales in a circle around a bonfire next to a large pond on a crisp, mid-October evening enjoying a potluck and having a great time socializing.

But this time, it was too painful for me to be there even though I was with my two sons. Ched wasn't sitting on the hay bale next to me as he always did warming my hands with his while we drank hot chocolate to stay warm. Ched wasn't there to tell his wonderful stories. An eerie silence permeated the party, but only in my own mind because something was missing and it was my dear life-partner. The reality of being without him was overwhelming my senses. I felt a chill in my body that was colder than the crisp breeze that fell upon all of us as we sat under the darkened moonlit and starry sky. I haven't been back since.

Another time my son told me that the members of the Triumph club were asking about me and wanted me to join them on one of their car cruises. We also had a vintage Triumph so my son talked me into going during the summer, a few months after Ched died. It was awkward walking up to the parking lot of the restaurant where we were meeting and everyone knew it, because Ched wasn't at my side. The people were very nice to me, of course, and the drive through the country was wonderful; but I felt anguished being without Ched.

A few times cell memory took over and while I was observing something in a corn field, I suddenly turned my head to look at Ched driving the car to tell him what I saw and then WHAM! It wasn't Ched; it was my son driving the car. A single tear fell from my eye to remind me of the reality I was experiencing. I felt both sadness and joy at the same time. Ched wasn't with me as he had been for so many years, driving together on these wonderful car cruises; but my precious son wanted me to once again enjoy the experience that had always meant so much to me. But even though at times it was painful for me not to see Ched driving the car, there were other moments when I felt very comforted in believing that Ched's spirit was there riding with us through the countryside.

I was once again experiencing the roller coaster emotions of missing Ched and the bond we shared riding together in our vintage Austin Healey sports car. Memories flooded my mind of the true joy we always felt when we were together like that. I recalled Ched's adventuresome spirit. He would come home from work a bit stressed and say, "Let's go; we need to air out."

I always knew that meant I was to stop whatever I was doing, get my scarf and sunglasses and we were off to places unknown, often times riding into the sunset and arriving home after dark.

He always wanted to explore new territory by saying, "Let's see where this road leads us," and then he would find another road and say the same thing. He loved to discover new places along our journey with his carefree attitude.

"Ched, do you know where you are going? We've been driving for a few hours already. Are we lost? We have no map, how will we get home?" I would ask in my inquisitive voice.

"We'll just follow the sun," he would casually say.

When I first heard him tell me that, I didn't understand what he meant. Having sailed on the Chesapeake Bay as a younger boy, he used the sun's position in the sky as his compass, indicative of the direction he wanted to sail. He used to reassure me when we were far from home with no map or GPS by telling me, "As long as you know how to navigate by the sun, you will always be able to find your way back home."

Ched could even tell what time it was by the sun's position. He would be off the time by only ten minutes or so. I was always amazed by that. He tried to teach me to be guided by the sun but I didn't do it as well as he could. Those wonderful memories became a harsh reality that I would never again experience that joy of riding with him in our Austin Healey or our Triumph or enjoying once more, the social activities of the car clubs to which we belonged. I realized that I might need a little more time before re-joining the car clubs; perhaps I never would, and that would be okay. My intuition will be my compass to direct me from unknown territories back to my own "home," to that inner place within me that will move me forward on my journey back toward acceptance and wholeness.

Dr. Elisabeth Kubler-Ross once talked about moving on into the unknown when she wrote, *"How do geese know when to fly to the sun? Who tells them the seasons? How do we, humans know when it is time to move on? As with the migrant birds, so surely with us, there is a voice within if only we would listen to it, that tells us certainly when to go forth into the unknown."*

My younger son Randy, told me that he, too, felt uncomfortable around the car club members and events because they were a painful reminder of how involved our family was at one time. He is considering selling his two vintage Austin Healeys, and is taking up fishing as his hobby in lieu of the car club activities.

My older son Chris, continues to enjoy the car club events. Every person's grief is unique. While Ched was still alive but could no longer drive, he gave our Austin Healey to Chris who worked alongside him to restore it to its pristine condition. To this day Chris still refers to it as "Dad's car." When I say, "No, it's yours," he always tells me, "As long as you are alive, Mom, it will always be Dad's and your car. I'm just temporarily responsible for it."

Time to Remove His Possessions

The computer room in our house has two roll-top desks, one for me and one for Ched. The walls on Ched's side of the room are filled with Austin Healey awards, memorabilia, and photos that meant so much to Ched. My side of the room also has many awards that I won as a result from participating in car rally competitions with my younger son Randy. He was the driver and I was the navigator, and we spent many summer weekends competing in the Central Ohio Rally Club competitions.

After many months went by, I began to feel the need to remove these reminders of the car events that meant so much to us, but I'm doing it very slowly. Over my desk I already removed some pencil sketch drawings of several MG sports cars and replaced them with my framed national book awards along with framed covers of the books I wrote and audio CDs I have recorded.

I will eventually remove Ched's items, giving the meaningful memorabilia to my sons to keep, and I will replace them with something that will make the room my own such as my cross-stitch projects, and some photos of cute baby animals which will bring a smile to my face when I look at them. Baby steps are required though; one step at a time. I will know when I am ready to lay to rest those external reminders of the wonderful sports car hobby we shared together. I can remove those personal items from sight but I will always retain the internal memories of that happy time we shared together. Death can never destroy my memories!

"Nothing is ever really lost to us as long as we remember them."

—L.M. Montgomery, The Story Girl

Grief Triggers

Shortly after Ched died, I discovered there were certain triggers that would immediately sky-rocket my grief emotions. The music on the radio soon became something I could not listen to. The songs were love songs with reminders of how much someone was loved, or missed. Occasionally, our song, "Unchained Melody" by the Righteous Brothers, the song we fell in love to during high school would play and I would burst out crying uncontrollably. I had to stop listening to the radio because the song lyrics were too emotional for me. Instead, I went to the library and checked out audio opera CDs which were sung in Italian by master artists such as Pavarotti, Domingo, Carreras, Bocelli, Russell Watson and others. I continue to this day not to listen to the radio, instead, playing soft New Age and opera music.

I still cannot eat at certain restaurants that Ched and I used to enjoy together. One time I went to a Chinese restaurant we always went to and it was very upsetting for me. In my mind's eye I could see Ched's face smiling at me, but at the same time I saw an empty chair and realized that I would never again enjoy having a nice dinner and conversation with him at one of our favorite restaurants. It was an awful experience to say the least, and I haven't tried again to go to the same restaurants we went to for that reason.

Even today, I still cannot drive past one restaurant we always went to after Ched's dialysis treatments. Seeing that restaurant brings up so many fresh memories. I want to help him sit in his chair because he is weak from his dialysis treatment. I want to observe his bandaged arm to make sure he wouldn't have a sudden rupture of the vein, something which is not uncommon following a dialysis treatment and necessitating an immediate trip to the ER. One of the dialysis patients died because his vein ruptured during the night and he bled to death in his sleep. I was always aware of any symptoms Ched might have following his dialysis treatments. I want to sit next to him in the restaurant and hear him talk about the dialysis nurses and how he made them laugh that day. I want to laugh again with him! Despite how sick he was at times, he never failed to make me laugh every single day. He gave me the gift of himself just by being with me whether he was sick or well.

So it is for that reason that this particular restaurant holds such intense memories for me and why it is still painful for me to drive past it. In order to not have to deal with that pain, I drive out of my way to approach the bank which is next door to the restaurant. I don't look at the restaurant when I am at the bank's drive-through window and that helps me to avoid that momentary pain.

I shared that story with someone and she looked at me as if I were crazy. Her eyebrows were squeezed together while her eyes evoked confusion and disbelief about what I told her.

"Nancy, why in the world do you feel that way? She asked. That's very strange!"

I replied, "The grief process is something you can never plan for or anticipate. Emotions suddenly appear and you just have to deal with them in the way that is best for you. Eventually, I am sure I will be able to drive past that restaurant, but not yet."

"Well, is there anything you can do so you won't feel so bad when you are driving past the restaurant?" she asked.

I replied, "I just told you how I manage to protect myself from the painful emotions that driving past the restaurant evokes for me. Other than that, there is nothing I can do except allow time to heal the sorrow I feel."

She shrugged her shoulders as if she still thought I was crazy and then she changed the subject.

Apparently she could not contemplate the pain and suffering of someone going through the process of grief, and my grief seemed strange to her. She could not relate to having had a very loving and long term relationship with a spouse that ended in death.

I am revealing with utmost honesty these seemingly unusual reactions that Ihave experienced. The grief process is an intense and *individually* shattering experience that will take time to sort out. Even the most confusing reactions during this period of grieving are normal even though we or our friends consider us to be crazy. We are not! We are in a state that is new and raw, and overwhelmingly painful and scary, so we shouldn't let anyone's reactions to us deter us from experiencing our sorrow **in our own, individual way.**

Being honest with my feelings of grief allows me to express my deepest, most intimate, and heartfelt expression of my love for Ched. When I abandon myself into my honest feelings, I am being driven blindly to find my place in life without Ched. Those emotions however brutal they may be, seem to have the ability to lift me momentarily out of myself, dissipating those painful emotions into the empty spaces surrounding me. It feels as if I can continue to live without myheart bursting. If no one can understand that or empathize with that, it's okay. This is something I am doing for myself, and not for others.

A Place of Comfort

Ched loved the white birch tree we planted by the pond many years ago so my sons and I scattered some of Ched's ashes beneath a large rock next to the tree. We also found a way to honor him by planting a memorial garden for him by that birch tree a few months after he died. My younger son Randy and I went to the nursery and chose shade hosta plants and other greenery that Ched loved. Randy did the heavy work of planting nearly forty large plants, carefully designed to create a beautiful area that blended with all my other shade plants. We placed stepping stones in a walking path through the adjoining plants and placed a memorial concrete bench seat with a beautiful inscription in it about losing and missing a loved one.

This particular area of my shade garden is not bothered by the deer who munch on all my other plants. It is as if they understand that this is off limits to them so that I can rest there and enjoy the loving memory of Ched among the host as and under the white birch tree that he loved so much. I am grateful that my son and I established this little sanctuary as it is a great comfort to me whenever I sit on the bench seat. I feel connected with Ched's spirit there and it helps to soothe my own spirit.

One warm and sunny May afternoon, I began pulling weeds from this garden. The previous evening it rained heavily so the ground was soft, making the chore of weed-pulling much easier to do. I have approximately one-quarter acre of garden beds that I planted among the tall ash trees. Lovely wooded paths smothered with decaying leaves meander throughout my garden beds outlining them and allowing for a pleasant walk throughout the shady garden and the woods.

I began this enormous gardening project when we moved to our home in 1972. At that time, the land was full of underbrush and weeds. Not a flower was to be seen anywhere. My love for gardening changed all that however, and I have created a nature paradise for my family and others to enjoy, including a fish pond with a waterfall that my son Randy built. By providing food, water, cover and a place for wildlife to raise their young, I qualified my land to become an official certified wildlife habitat by the National Wildlife Federation.

On this particular day, the warm sun was peeking through the tree tops and occasionally breaking through to cast light upon the ground. After pulling weeds for several hours, I needed a break. *Should I sit on one of the wooden benches along the paths,* or perhaps lie on the hammock? I wondered. No, I will sit with Ched on the bench seat by the white birch tree.

My spirit naturally connected with Ched. *Hello Ched, I've come to sit with you for a while. The hostas are growing so nicely this year, aren't they? Did you see how many times the pileated woodpecker has visited our ash trees? I remember that you once told me that they eat the insects in the bark of the trees. Well, you were correct. We now have a huge problem with the Emerald Ash Borer. The insect is burrowing into the bark of our ash trees, and cutting off the nutrition to the trees. The trees are dying now, Ched.*

If you were still with us, you would know what to do about the trees, but I have to make those decisions now. I hired a tree service to cut down some of the trees close to the house in the event they would collapse onto the house and damage it. Randy has been cutting down other dead ash trees that are farther into the woods and splitting them for firewood so I can burn it in our wood-burning stove. There will be more dying ash trees to cut down, but Randy will cut them down as needed. You would be proud of me, Ched. I am burning the wood as my primary heat source in the cold winter months so I don't have to use so much expensive home heating fuel oil.

I hate seeing our ash trees dying. I cry for them. They once stood tall and watched over us, providing us with summer's cooling shade. It's another reminder to me that life doesn't continue forever, and all things must eventually die. But it is hard to watch death approach and take from us the gift of life that was given to us. You were that gift to us, Ched!

It is still hard for me at times to realize that death took you from us. There are moments when I am in the house when I can feel your presence so strongly. I turn my head to look at you but you aren't there. Yet, I know you are there! I feel your love wash over me, bathing me as it lifts me into a new and expanded awareness of your presence with me. Your love comes in such a soft way, penetrating through the strongest barriers to get to me. Every time I sense your presence, I feel so blessed, for that truly is the power of love! Even though my eyes cannot see you Ched, I see you in my heart where your spirit glows deep within me- that eternal expression of your love within me.

The forest will renew itself in time Ched, but I will no longer be here to enjoy its beauty. I am getting old myself and one day, I will return to your arms. In the meantime, I will come and sit with you here, by the white birch tree where you lie. Randy has already placed another large rock next to your rock for me to rest with you. God-willing, the birch tree will live for many, many years. If not, at least for the time being, it brings me the serenity that comforts me. I love you, my darling!"

Coping With Holidays

Holidays are generally time spent with those we love. They can be the most difficult parts of the grieving process because our loved one is not with us during those times of celebration. Who wants to celebrate when our personal loss is so heartbreaking? It is natural to feel that we would like to sleep through the holiday and wake up when it's over. I dreaded the first Thanksgiving holiday, but my sons were also grieving and I felt it was important that we should be together for our usual turkey dinner with all the trimmings even though we were in so much pain. I placed Ched's photo at the head of the table where he customarily sat for dinner. In my heart I knew his spirit was with us, and this was comforting to me whenever I gazed at his photo.

My sons also felt it was an appropriate way to honor Ched by inviting his spirit to join us at the table. We were also able to laugh when we shared some memories of Ched. There is no right or wrong way to navigate through a holiday, but we were able to get through that first Thanksgiving just by being together and sharing our love for one another. It was still important to share our bond as family.

Christmas was a very different story however. When the Christmas cards started arriving, I opened only a few of them. Everyone was wishing me "Happy Holidays." Some friends were saying, "I hope you have a great New Year." The cards were depressing me; they were not cheering me up. I couldn't stand to open another card and find the same cheerful messages saying, "I hope your holidays are wonderful."

How can they be wonderful, I thought. My husband died and he is not here with his family to celebrate Christmas with us. Don't you people understand what I am going through on this first Christmas without him? No, I guess you don't, otherwise you wouldn't have sent me those cards to remind me how impossible it is to be "happy" at this time of the year.

Why did I feel so angry when my dear friends were being nice to me by sending me Christmas cards just as they did every year? I felt awful for feeling that anger. I love my friends and they love me. Sending me a Christmas card was their way of connecting with me during that joyful season. But those cards were depressing me by making my loss seem even more unbearable at this particular time of the holiday season because Ched had died.

Any cards I received after those few – whether from family or friends, out of town or local – were never opened. They went straight into the trash. I didn't send any Christmas cards to anyone either. I did receive a card from a friend, though, which was not a Christmas card at all. It was a "thinking of you at this diffi-cult time" card which was *very much appreciated*. She understood what I must have been feeling during the Christmas season and didn't feel that one of those standard "Happy Holidays" Christ-mas cards was appropriate for me. Bless her heart!

It's okay not to put up a Christmas tree. It's okay not to deco-rate. I didn't and I don't plan on doing that ever again. I did, however, place a battery operated solar angel lantern outdoors under the white birch tree that Ched loved. At night it glows with the outline of the angel and it's lovely to see it when I peek out from my bedroom window.

I don't have grandchildren to buy presents for, but I did purchase some toys for our local Toys For Tots charity drive so underprivileged children could be visited by Santa Claus and receive some toys. And once again, my sons and I gathered together for a wonderful meal that I prepared and we sat at the dinner table with Ched's photo at the head of the table.

I am not looking forward to Christmases without Ched, but I expect my grief to soften in the coming years and I will be able to move through Christmas a little easier as time goes on. I am giving myself permission to take baby steps through the grieving process, holidays included.

Daily Adjustments

"Sometimes the hardest part isn't letting go but rather learning to start over."
—Nicole Sobon

I wasn't prepared for the new role that was suddenly thrust upon me that forced me to redefine myself and my role in life. The partnership that Ched and I had was composed of our strengths and weaknesses. Fortunately for us, my weaknesses were Ched's strengths, and my strengths were Ched's weaknesses. Together, we made a great team. Ched had exceptional skills in logic and math so he took care of all the various household tasks that required those skills. I am the last person you want to trust balancing a checkbook so Ched took care of all the family finances. Now I have that responsibility and while I continue to make mistakes every month balancing the checkbook, my son will shake his head with disbelief and simply correct the mistakes for me without scolding me for it. Bless his heart!

*"When you come to the edge of all the light you have known
and are about to step out into the darkness, Faith is knowing one of two things will happen... There will be something
to stand on or you will be taught how to fly."*

—Author unknown

I am learning about myself every day. I find I am becoming more assertive, expressing my needs and feelings to those
who are being inconsiderate. I do not want to be rude, but I am
taking care of myself in this way as a loving thing I can do for
myself. Allowing others' insensitive remarks to imprint upon my
mind could do more harm on my path toward healing. I am also
taking the time to genuinely and with heartfelt gratitude thank
those individuals who convey their kind words to me. I know
they appreciate it, as well as I do.

I also realize that it is important to remain appreciative of
the good things in my life despite my grief. I live in a beautiful wooded setting where I can enjoy my natural surroundings.
Nature has always been food for my soul and this is something I
will not allow my grief to destroy. I make it a point to go outdoors
every time the weather permits, either to work in my garden or
simply to sit and listen to the beautiful, comforting sounds of
nature. This is where I feel God's presence with me most closely.
Even when I am crying as I am gazing into the fish pond, I can
feel as if God is wrapping me in a warm, fuzzy blanket of comfort. This is very soothing to my soul and reminds me that I am
not alone, even though at times, I think I am.

The human spirit is nourished by nature. When I listen to
the teachings of nature itself - the breeze, the sound of a waterfall,
the rustle of crisp Autumn leaves, I am offered times of contem-
plation and reflection which remind me of the world's renewal
and my own. This allows me to shift my mood into a lighter place.

While I am grieving, it is very important to trust that I can still have a hopeful attitude about whatever lies ahead. To remain hopeful doesn't mean I will stop missing Ched. I will never stop missing him! But I have a purpose to my life and part of that purpose is being open to the changing beauty that comes from within as I move through my journey of grief and through my journey of life as well. Being open to fully embrace the changes I have yet to make shows me there will be a way through my suffering while finding meaning to my life. It will be my struggles that will reveal the triumph of my strengths.

> *"As long as I can I will look at this world for both of us. As long as I can I will laugh with the birds, I will sing with the flowers, I will pray to the stars, for both of us."*
>
> —Sascha

5

Good Grief

"We bereaved are not alone. We belong to the largest company in all the world – the company of those who have known suffering."

—Helen Keller

I am still very vulnerable. My emotions are on the surface at all times; they call out to me to deal with them. Life is moving on without Ched and as much as I want life to stand still, it won't. I am transitioning into unknown as well as familiar territory and sometimes I question if I am ready to make that transition. I realize that although Ched is missing, the life he left behind for Chris, Randy, and me was his gift to us. But I still don't know how to say good-bye to Ched, the love of my life.

This is my reality even when I feel as if I am still dreaming and hoping that when I wake up, Ched will still be here. But he is not. Sometimes, for just a moment, I can sense his presence with me. It is a very strong and comforting feeling. Intuitively, I know he is aware of me and wants me to regain that lost part of myself that was part of him when he was alive. *How will I do that?* I ask myself, still frozen in that time when we were a couple.

There are daily reminders on television or when I go shopping that Ched and I are no longer a couple. When I see couples engaged in everyday activities, I see a reflection in them of the couple that Ched and I once were. I think of the happy times when we attended social events, when we danced, when we went shopping, or when Ched told his stories to people he just met – stories I heard a hundred times, but I still enjoyed hearing them. I look at other couples, especially older ones and think how fortunate they are to be together as couples. Silently, I say to them, "Cherish one another."

No one can stand alone in this journey through grief. As horrendous as this challenge is, each has help, both seen and unseen. A friend of mine whose husband was tragically killed when his car went off the road and into a pond called me one day. She invited me to join the "Good Grief Dinner Club." Once a month individuals whose spouses had died met for dinner at a country club for socialization.

"This is such a nice group Nancy," my friend told me. "It gives us an excuse to get dressed up once a month and go out to a fancy place for dinner; why don't you come with us?"

"I would like that." I replied.

"Great. I'll pick you up at 5:30 pm and we'll head over to Scioto Country Club where we will enjoy a wonderful dinner and meet new people." She replied.

I didn't know what to expect. *Was I ready to socialize with others whose spouses had died? What do you talk about? What is the demeanor of the group?* I wondered.

Walking into the large ballroom where the event was taking place, I saw that the room was filled with men and women seated at round tables adorned with crisp white tablecloths and fresh flowers. My immediate reaction was an overwhelming sense of compassion for all these men and women that numbered from 75-100. I realized that each of them had lost their spouse just as I had, and I felt an intimate connection with them even though they were complete strangers to me.

My friend found a table for us with some of her friends and soon I felt at ease and happy that I came. We had a wonderful, light-hearted evening with men and women talking and laughing together. I haven't missed one Good Grief Dinner outing since then.

I have gained the perspective that it is important to nurture quality relationships and know the importance of being connected with others. Friends, family, and faith are an unbeatable combination of support for any crisis.

Every day I must strike a balance between taking an active role in my life, and surrendering to the mystery of life, including my temporary setbacks. I realize that the winds of change are all around me and there is no quick fix to rebuild my life. But I have also come to understand that the brilliant light that illuminated my life will not – must not be forgotten.

I have tried to show how insensitive comments, though well-meaning, can be absorbed into a grieving person's heart, making the sorrow worse. In writing about this I hope to bring attention to misguided attempts at comfort and spare another heartbroken person from having to suffer needlessly. Those who are dealing with loss have enough to deal with. This is one of the most important lessons my own loss has taught me – what *not* to say to someone in deep emotional pain. I believe that using my grief to help others helps me as well.

6

Caring Souls

"Some people come into our lives and leave footprints on our hearts and we are never ever the same again."

—Flavia Weedn

November 21, 2011

It was the first Thanksgiving after Ched died and I started the week with my usual feelings of missing Ched. I sent a Thanksgiving Day card to the dialysis center who took care of Ched (and me) for the past 5 years. It was a heartfelt expression of my appreciation for all they did for Ched and for me, and I wanted them to know that I was feeling so much gratitude for them on this particular Thanksgiving holiday. I felt good after I sent it off in the mail knowing they would appreciate my thinking of them especially during my time of grief.

I decided to go to the grocery store to get some ingredients for Thanksgiving Day dinner. I had tried doing that days earlier and spent four unproductive hours feeling lost shopping for ingredients that I had no desire to purchase. So I returned to try again on the Monday before Thanksgiving Day.

Walking up and down the aisles, the Christmas music playing

over the speakers, I was beginning to feel lost again. I didn't want to do this!!! But I had to do something for Thanksgiving for my sons to enjoy, or at least to eat a good meal – just the three of us. My sons and I needed to be together to share our sorrow and our memories. We needed to laugh, we needed to cry, and we needed to continue to love one another. We needed to remember that family is the most important thing there is even though one member was no longer with us.

Three hours later, my shopping basket was filled with the ingredients for the Thanksgiving dinner and I was ready to go home. *But one more stop*, I thought. I would stop at Trader Joe's, a small natural food store, and check out their selection of fish. I always loved their fish; but I wasn't cooking for myself anymore, so I wondered why in the world I was going there! *Oh well, maybe I'll see something. Who knows?* I felt sort of on cruise control, not really slowing down or stopping to find a reason for driving to Trader Joe's grocery store. I just went.

Okay, I was browsing the shelves at Trader Joe's, enjoying the free cup of hot cider, but I didn't see anything I wanted to buy. Whoops! The fresh flowers were nice! I took a look at them. There was one bunch that had three yellow rose buds in the bouquet. Ched always bought me yellow roses for special occasions because they are my favorite flower. He was always so considerate of me that way. There were two white roses and some other flowers in the bouquet. But when I saw those yellow rose buds, I knew I had to buy them just to remember Ched on Thanksgiving Day.

I felt so sad when I plucked them out of the vase they were soaking in. So many memories of yellow roses he always gave me for special occasions and now, I found that now I was buying them for myself. I missed Ched so much!!! I swallowed hard and reminded myself I was in a public store. I had to remain cool, calm and collected.

I proceeded to the checkout counter where I placed the bouquet of flowers on the counter and began to get the $4.26 from my wallet. The young cashier asked me if I was buying them for someone special.

"No, I'm just buying them for myself." I said softly.

He asked me if I was buying them for myself to cheer myself up and I said "Yes."

As I placed my money in his hands and he was ringing up the sale, he asked me if I was having a bad day.

I said, "Yes, I am having a very bad day."

As if that wasn't enough for this young man, he asked me why I was having a bad day and I told him that my husband recently died and I was not looking forward to Thanksgiving without him.

At that point, he handed me the bouquet of flowers and said, "These are for you; we want you to have them on us."

I must have had a shocked look on my face because he repeated what he said and added that he would not accept my money.

"No, no," I responded, "you must accept my money."

He insisted, "No, I won't accept your money. These flowers are for you."

I was so emotional at that point, realizing that this young man would have that much compassion for a stranger whose husband had died and who was not looking forward to Thanksgiving without him. I began to tear up but held it in, thanking him for what he did for me. When I got outside the store, the dam broke and I cried and cried. I had to sit in my car for awhile until I was able to drive home. The flood of gratitude for the simple act of kindness from this young man was overwhelming.

While driving home, I thought of all the people who wanted me to stop thinking about Ched and move on with my life; who judged my feelings and wanted to fix me with their wisdom and with their faith. This young man did none of that; yet he did more for me than all those friends who were impatient with my grief process.

My yellow roses that Ched always gave me for special occasions were placed on our Thanksgiving dining room table and in a real sense, God, the universe, synchronicity, whatever you wish to call it, saw to it that someone's spiritual arms wrapped around me and provided a lift for my spirit in a way that I couldn't have imagined. I will always remember what that compassionate young cashier did for me that day to help ease my pain during the first Thanksgiving holiday without Ched.

A Friend Who Understands

A year and a half after my husband's death, a friend who lives in California sent me a book in the mail that was written by a woman whose husband had died. My friend's note simply said, "Here's someone's story you will be able to relate to." The book was titled, *It's All Right, I'm Only Crying*, by Kathleen Christison.

Reading that woman's story helped me to feel as if someone else understood the pain I was going through. Many of my well-intentioned friends had no clue as to what I was going through. But Kathleen Christison knew what that pain was like! I felt an immediate connection or bond with her and her story. It was at that time when I realized how much value there was in reading someone else's *personal story of grief* and how it allowed me to FEEL my own grief.

There are many books written on the subject of grief and loss written by experts in the field of psychology, social work, and other fields. But those books *for me* were rather boring to read. They were written in a clinical manner with lots of good information, but I couldn't relate to them in a personal manner. Often times I asked myself, *Did this author ever personally experience profound grief himself, or was he simply writing about grief based upon the professional expertise in counseling others who were going through it?*

While those books were not helpful to me, they can be of enormous help to someone else! People have different and unique needs when experiencing the most devastating heartbreak of all- the loss of a loved one – and they should seek out any resource that feels helpful.

I was so deeply touched by my friend's kindness when he sent me Kathleen Christison's book because he instinctively knew that reading someone else's *personal* story in a book would be a point of *connection* for me that would help me to explore my own loss in its entirety. My friend's loving gesture taught me that these are moments of *love in action*, and are the times during the grief process when one's spirit is lifted beyond the sadness of the moment because of the kindness of another.

"When we honestly ask ourselves which person in our lives means the most to us, we find that it is those who share our pain and touch our words with a gentle and tender hand, the friend who can be silent with us in a moment of despair or confusion, who can stay with us in an hour of grief and bereavement, who can tolerate not knowing, not curing, not healing and face with us the reality of our powerlessness, that is a friend who cares."

—Henri Nouwen

A Purposeful Encounter

The silence in the house is sometimes more than I can bear, especially during the cold winter months when there aren't many outside activities to do. There are times when I have to get out of the house and just walk around the stores, window shop, or buy something I don't need. At least I see people; at least I can speak to a cashier when they say, "Have a nice day." At least I can feel the harsh winter wind on my face and know that I am still alive, putting one foot in front of the other and moving forward somehow.

One day I needed to go shopping at Anderson's store to buy a large funnel that Chris could use in the garage when he was working on his car. When he needed to use a funnel, he usually came into the kitchen and took mine for his use. Naturally, I wouldn't use that funnel again, so I wanted to get him one for his own garage use.

Approaching a traffic light traveling eastbound, all of a sudden, I turned the steering wheel and made a left hand turn at the traffic light and headed toward Golden Corral Restaurant. I thought, *Why in the world did I turn the car here? I have no plans to eat at this restaurant.* But then I thought, *Well Nancy, go ahead and eat at the restaurant. You need to eat some vegetables.*

I rarely cook for myself anymore. Once I was a gourmet cook, loving those times when Ched and I would enjoy a good meal together. But it isn't the same anymore so I just eat something from the refrigerator that I can pick up easily. When my sons visit me, I will prepare a nice meal for us to enjoy, and then I will have some leftovers to put in the refrigerator for my next meals.

As I was driving in the parking lot of the Golden Corral Restaurant, I had convinced myself that I needed to go inside to eat some veggies, I thought, so the decision to go into the restaurant was for that reason, even though I had not planned on going there.

Once inside the restaurant, I chose a table and took off the beautiful wolf jacket my son Chris bought me one year when he was in Minnesota. Every time I wear it, it seems someone compliments me on it. I sat down at the table and noticed that an elderly couple sat down at an adjacent table. As the woman walked past me to go to the buffet tables, she said to me, "I love your sweatshirt with all the birds on it- it's so lovely! And I just love your jacket – it's so unusual!" I thanked her for the compliment and told her it was very kind of her to say that.

Since they were seated directly in front of me, our eyes touched each other's occasionally and we both acknowledged a smile. I was drinking my coffee and nearly finished with my meal when suddenly a very strong ray of sunlight zeroed into my eyes, making me squint. At that moment, the woman said to me, "That sun is right in your eyes; do you want to join us at our table?"

I replied, "No thank you, I'm almost ready to leave."

Throughout our lunch, I couldn't help notice that they were very much in love. Sweet gestures they made to one another were so endearing to watch. We began a conversation. Because it was very noisy in the room and I couldn't hear everything that was being said, I got up from my table, put my jacket on and went over to their table to speak to them.

I learned that he was a retired ophthalmologist who practiced in the same building where I go for my eye care. They told me that they would soon be celebrating their 23rd wedding anniversary. As they spoke, they immediately grabbed each other's hands and held them tenderly. *Oh, how sweet,* I thought.

I told them my story of how I met Ched and that we had been married for 49 years before he died. I related the story of how he died, and they listened intently with no indication that they didn't want to hear my story. They allowed me to speak from my heart and tell them about the greatest love of my life. Their eyes sparkled with compassion and an occasional tear fell from the woman's eye. After telling my story, I told them how fortunate they are to love one another so deeply. She then began to tell me about their own love story while I listened intently.

Suddenly, she said, "Listening to our love story must be so hard for you because it must remind you of what you had but no longer have."

Ouch! That was exactly how I felt! I swallowed hard, not allowing my tears to well up in my eyes.

Somehow while we were talking about death, I happened to mention that I died once during childbirth and had a near-death experience. She was taken aback and said, "I had a near-death experience during childbirth as well!"

We talked for ten minutes more about our near-death experiences and how significant they were to our spirituality. "Nancy, she said, "having had a near-death experience, why that must be such a comfort to you now that your husband died."

"Yes," I replied, not wanting to expound any further on how my near-death experience could not possibly replace the grief that I was feeling. I simply changed the subject quickly.

Before any tears could well up in my eyes, I told them I had to leave. I was pleasantly surprised when both of them grabbed my hands and held them as if they didn't want me to go. We could have spent hours talking, but it was time for me to leave.

The woman gazed into my eyes and said, "We both noticed that you appeared lonely sitting at your table by yourself. I hope you feel better now that you had a chance to talk with us. You are such a lovely woman, Nancy. We would love to join you for lunch again anytime you want to get together again."

We exchanged contact information and then I left them to enjoy their lunch together without interruption. I floated out of the restaurant on a cloud of joy. My day began with feelings of loneliness and became transformed into a blessed day. I knew when my steering wheel suddenly made a left turn into the parking lot of the restaurant that I was meant to share a few moments with a wonderful couple who lifted my spirits. My next stop was to go to Anderson's to buy a large funnel for Chris.

"There are three needs of the griever: To find the words for the loss, to say the words aloud and to know that the words have been heard."

—Victoria Alexander

Laughter Is Good Medicine

"In the sweetness of friendship let there be laughter, and sharing of pleasures. For in the dew of little things the heart finds its morning and is refreshed."

—Kahlil Gibran

I wrote earlier that I loved to laugh with Ched. After he died, I missed that so much! In spite of the raw pain of my grief, there were occasions when laughter momentarily lifted me. A dear friend of mine has a wonderful sense of humor. On occasion, he emailed me funny photos of animals or jokes he thought I might appreciate.

Well, I did appreciate them! I laughed so hard at times that my stomach hurt. This was a friend who once told me he didn't know what to say or do to comfort me after Ched died. But he sent me emails to help me laugh again and lightened my burden. Sometimes I emailed him and told him how I handled a problem around the house by myself and how I usually failed at solving it. His reply was usually suggesting a Plan C which was a comical solution to my problem and one that would make me laugh so hard! That humor helped me to go easy on myself when I became frustrated with myself when attempting to fix a household problem that Ched would have taken care of easily. I am so grateful to Mark for thinking of me in this way. He is indeed, helping me to feel refreshed for a few moments with the laughter that I still need to enjoy. He is a perfect example of someone who doesn't judge my grief, lecture me or tell me how to stop grieving. Instead, he is supporting me with his humor because he knows I need to laugh again.

7

Going Home

"Death…is not more than passing from one room into another. But there's a difference for me, you know. Because in that other room I shall be able to see."

—Helen Keller

When people are close to death or have died and been resuscitated, they often report that the "self" has left the physical body and is hovering overhead witnessing the resuscitation process from above and other events taking place. They report traveling at a fast rate of speed and passing through a portal and into the presence of a Being of light radiating unearthly unconditional love beyond what the human mind can imagine. They often meet deceased loved ones before returning back to physical consciousness. Such experiences are called near-death experiences.

I was at Heaven's door twice, and if I spent the remainder of my life trying to find the words to communicate what those experiences were like, I would fail because there are not enough words in the human language to describe them. It is like trying to describe a color to a blind person. But I can truthfully say that death is not an ending, but a new beginning; a transition to an afterlife of immense joy.

As a result of my near-death and near-death-like experiences I have been very active in teaching and writing books. My intention is to help others realize there is life after death, and that the meaning and purpose of our lives is to learn the importance of being a loving human being while we have the opportunity here on earth. In 1984, I formed a chapter of the International Association for Near-Death Studies (IANDS) in Columbus, Ohio and continue to serve as its president. The purpose is to provide support to those who have had spiritually transformative experiences and to provide information about these experiences to the general public. Through writing and speaking, I am fulfilling my promise to the Light of God to serve in the manner I was called. My book, *Hear His Voice: The Light's Message for Humanity: Revelations From a Woman Who Came Back From Heaven's Door Twice* earned a national award for the amazing story of my encounters with the Light of God.

The riches that are imprinted in my heart and soul as a result of having been at Heaven's door twice are vast, and my gratitude will remain forever. But just as there are two sides of a coin, there are two sides to my journey through grief. When my thoughts shift to where Ched is and what he is experiencing, I can feel some release from the awful nightmare that my grief entails.

I recall the memories of what my near-death and near-death-like experiences were like and I know that Ched is now experiencing the bliss that I also experienced. For that reason I am happy for him. Now he knows for himself all that I tried to convey to him for so many years with words that were foreign and meaningless to him when he was alive on earth. He was a full-blown skeptic and believed that when we die, its light's out, period, end of story. I am comforted now in knowing he lives again, although in another form and that he is very, very happy!

But the other side of the coin is that even though I have treasures within me from my Sacred encounters with the Creator, those treasures do NOT insulate me from the pain of my loss. There is a presumption on the part of so many people that because I was once with the Light of God during my near-death and near-death-like experiences, that somehow those experiences should shield me from grief. Generally, someone's comment to me would go something like this:

"Well Nancy, you of all people should know that Ched is now in Heaven. You know that he is with God; you've been there yourself, so you shouldn't be sad."

Nonsense! I know where he is. I'm not grieving for him – I'm grieving for ME! I still cry my eyes out – seemingly endlessly. I still miss him like crazy. I still long for his touch or the sound of his voice. I still want to fulfill all the hopes and dreams we envisioned. But those hopes and dreams are gone forever. I lost a companion who brought me love, joy, comfort, tolerance, respect, balance, and meaning to my life in ways that are unique, admirable, and worthy of remembering.

As long as I am a human being living in this earthly realm, I will embrace both the pain of separation as well as the realization that life goes on one way or another. My sorrow is the result of being a fully evolved human being, one who has loved deeply and completely, a human being who knows about loss, but also the life lived. Even though my encounters with our Creator and the unconditional love I was graced with were the most supreme experiences of my entire life, the death of my beloved soul-mate revealed to me the ultimate unconditional love that one human being can have for another. When that love ceases to be shared with another, one can only long for its return, but it is gone. The heart endures the loss of that love but continues to search for it even when it knows it has abandoned you. This is the pain I speak about. It leaves you unable to reclaim that most precious love that once was yours. It has vanished. My Heavenly experiencescannot bring back Ched's love to me in my daily life, but only as a memory. But I will cling to the faith that Ched and I will be reunited when my own life is over and that knowledge brings me great solace. It will be a wonderful reunion!

> *"What we call life is a journey to death. What we call death is the gateway to life."*
>
> —Anonymous

8

After-Death Contacts

"Do not weep, for I shall be more useful to you after my death and I shall help you then more effectively than during my life."

—St. Dominic

While I respect everyone's right to their own beliefs, I do not intend to try and persuade anyone in believing something they are uncomfortable with. I simply want to share information with others and if this information is helpful, fine. If not, that's okay too. Everyone must decide for themselves what they want to accept as their truth.

I want to make you aware of an article written by John Hooper on January 31, 1999 and published by the London Observer. In the article, The Rev. Gino Concetti, chief theological commentator for the Vatican newspaper, stated that the Catholic Church believes that communication with the dead is possible. Concetti states, "Communication is possible between those who live on this earth and those who live in a state of eternal repose, in heaven or purgatory. It may even be that God lets our loved ones send us messages to guide us at certain times in our life."

This attitude of the Catholic Church is based upon their belief in a "Communion of Saints," which includes Christians on earth as well as those in the afterlife. Concetti states, "Where there is communion, there is communication."

After Death Communications (ADCs)

The term "after-death communications" or "ADCs" was first coined by Bill and Judy Guggenheim who collected more than 3,300 accounts of individuals who were contacted by a deceased loved one without the use of a psychic, medium, ritual or device. Their excellent book, *Hello From Heaven!* has remained the most frequently read book on the subject. It is an exceptional contribution to the bereaved, offering comfort and hope that their loved ones are still with us in spirit and can communicate with us. I highly recommend it.

In a 1981 Gallup poll, 42% of Americans polled said they had contact with a departed loved one. Widows and widowers reported as high as 70 to 80 percent, while 75% of parents who lost a child had contact with their deceased child. These figures may even be higher because many people are afraid to mention them to anyone for fear of ridicule. But the more we speak about these experiences, the more we can add to the growing body of knowledge of the afterlife and of the nature of reality itself. When enough information is brought forth, a critical mass will take place and it will turn the unfamiliar into the familiar and lessen our fears. At the very least, such information can be immensely comforting and healing.

Sometimes I ask myself if my near-death and near-death-like experiences provided some comfort or lessened the pain I felt when Ched died. After all, my journey to Heaven's door to be with the Light of God was so incredibly beautiful that I never wanted to leave and return to earth. My answer is always absolutely NO, the experiences did not lessen the pain of Ched's death. While they did reassure me that Ched is now enjoying the Light of God as I did, and I am happy about that, it did not shield me from the pain of losing him.

And sometimes I ask myself another question. Did the after-death communications that I received from Ched help to lessen the suffering? The answer to that one is YES!

While it is true that people who have not had a near-death experience would be comforted by the knowledge of such experiences, that knowledge alone cannot heal the void that is left when relationships end. They may believe that their loved ones continue to live again after physical death; and they may have no doubt that they are experiencing bliss, but their loved ones are gone nonetheless and no longer a part of their lives.

The evidence of after-death communications, however, changes things. Information about these encounters, whether personally experienced or not, provides hope for the continuation of a relationship. Communication from beyond death's door is far more comforting because it allows the grieving to realize that the deceased loved ones are **still with them.**

Just reading about these ADC stories can bring healing in a far more personal way. The awareness of ADCs naturally causes people to pay more attention to the "signs" that their loved ones' spirits are nearby; they are less likely to disregard them as coincidences and more inclined to feel grateful. In other words, after-death-communications validate that a **connection** has been made with loved ones who have passed, and **that** is what is comforting to a grieving person!

Let's take a look at some of the ways several deceased friends and loved ones have contacted me. They are examples of *evidential after-death communications* in which a person conveys something that wasn't known previously, and had no way of knowing. Evidential after-death communications are very strong indicators that these encounters with deceased spirits are genuine communications and not hallucinations or meaningless dreams.

The deceased loved one is able to relay information that was not known to anyone but is later verified.

Promise Me

In a particular dream, I was in a German concentration camp walking alongside another woman. We were herded into a building and just before the door locked, she pushed me out and said, "Tell Jake that I'm very happy, and above all, tell him it's alright for him to find happiness again. Do you promise to do that for me?" With my eyes tenderly looking into hers, I said, "I promise." At that same moment someone slammed the door shut and locked it, leaving her inside as I stood outside the building. The dream ended.

Two days later my husband came home from work and announced that his friend Jake's wife died. I didn't know her and only casually knew Jake as a co-worker of my husband. We went to the funeral service and while the minister was delivering the eulogy, he mentioned she was Italian and proceeded to describe the life she had led while living in Italy and then later when she married Jake.

Listening politely to the minister's words, I heard him say something that would rattle the bones inside of me. He recalled a time in her life when she had spent time in a German concentration camp. Shocked by what I had just heard, I immediately thought of my dream and my promise to Jake's wife. I wondered how I would tell him and when. Would he think I was crazy if I talked about my dream with him? It is not easy to step out in faith and assume everyone will believe what I tell him or her, especially when it deals with the unobservable reality. I was very reluctant to tell him the day of her funeral, so I didn't.

Several months later, my husband and I attended his company's Christmas party. Coincidentally, seated at our table directly across from us were Jake and his female guest. Both of them, in their late sixties, held hands and talked intimately like sweet lovebirds to one another. It was apparent they were very much in love. I knew it was now or never. I had to tell Jake about my dream. Excusing myself from the table, I told Ched I was going to talk with Jake for a little while. Nervously, I knelt down beside Jake and took his hand in mine and said, "Jake, I'm going to tell you something, and you may dismiss what I'm going to say as being fanatical, lunacy or whatever, but I have to tell you."

I proceeded to tell him that his wife appeared to me in a dream and made me promise to tell him she is very happy and above all, she wants him to find happiness again. When Jake heard that, he spontaneously burst into tears. I looked at Ched sitting across from us and he had a wrinkled brow that said, "What did you do to Jake to make him cry?" With his eyes, Ched motioned me to come back to my chair but I knew I had to stay with Jake a few moments longer.

Jake pressed his hands over mine and cried, "Oh God, this is a miracle happening! You did the right thing by telling me. I can't thank you enough."

He proceeded to tell me that during the summer after his wife died, he went back to his high school reunion in Iowa. At that time, he met the woman who was seated beside him at the Christmas party. Apparently, they had been high school lovers and hadn't seen one another since then. She never married because Jake had been her only true love. She and Jake married shortly afterward.

Looking into my eyes, his eyes soaked with tears, Jake told me, "You had no idea I was dealing with a lot of guilt because I married so quickly after my wife's death. I felt guilty about finding happiness with another woman and it was tearing me up inside."

He went on to say that he now believed that his wife was bringing him a message from the beyond to let him know that it's okay to be happy. Jake was elated and his tear-filled eyes expressed such gratitude to me for sharing this message with him. That evening his guilt was replaced with genuine freedom to love again and to be loved. A healing had indeed taken place that evening, and I felt privileged to have witnessed and honored it.

I Saved the Last Dance for You

At one time in my young life, I was an Arthur Murray dance instructor. My partner, BG, was a wonderful human being whose life greatly impacted mine. When I moved to Ohio, BG and his wife moved to Texas, and we lost touch with one another except for the exchange of Christmas cards every year.

On May 29, 1988, I had a wonderful dream about BG. We were dancing once again all the glorious dances that we had performed together as partners in the early 1960's. The rhythmic Latin dances like the mambo, tango, samba, cha cha and rhumba; the graceful, fluid motions of the Viennese waltz, the foxtrot and the rigorous moves of the quickstep and swing - we danced them all in my dream.

What a thrilling experience it was to discover (in my dream) that I possessed all the balance, control, and rhythm that I once had as a spry young woman. We whirled around the dance floor as a single unit of energy, the way Fred Astaire and Ginger Rogers magically danced together. I felt exhilarated beyond words. You see, I stopped dancing completely when I moved to Ohio, and now all that remains is only a dim memory of that happy time in my life.

But here I was in my dream, dancing with my partner as if the interim years never existed. Time stood still for a few brief moments. We were having a marvelous time dancing together when suddenly he said to me, "I have to go now; I won't be back again. I won't see you anymore, but I wanted to save the last dance for you. But the dance of all dances has been my life shared with my wife all these years. I have been very happy with her. I am going to be okay so don't worry about me. I have to go now, I love you." I hugged him with the biggest hug possible, and then he walked away, and I awoke from the dream.

It was May 30, Memorial Day. I had not made any plans to celebrate the holiday because my family and I were very busy rebuilding our home after a fire completely destroyed it. We were spending all available time working at the job site. Yet, I awoke from my dream in such a festive mood, as if I were actually celebrating something. I kept thinking how special that dream was because it was so vivid and so **real**. All day long, my body felt deliriously energized by the dancing we did together in my dream, as if all my cells still retained those past memories. I was so enthralled to have danced again with BG even if it was "only a dream."

All day long, the energy impacted me in such a profound way that even when I was hammering nails or carrying the lumber, I performed those tasks with such love and joy in my heart. Why I even kicked up my heels a few times when no one was looking and whirled around the grass clutching an old broom for a dance partner. On a holiday when I couldn't spare the time to celebrate, in some quiet secret way, I was truly celebrating the love of my special friend BG, and the common love of the dance that we shared together so many years earlier.

Three months later, I received a note from BG's wife informing me **that he had died on May 30** from lung cancer. There is no doubt in my mind that love continues to exist beyond space and time. Love never dies! Love will always find its way to us, even in death.

Nancy, Help Me!

For several years my favorite hair stylist was a young woman in her early twenties who worked at a salon that I frequented. In the course of our friendship, we developed a trust and confidence that allowed us to talk freely about matters of our hearts. Since I am very active in the field of near-death experience studies, it was natural for me to share this information with her.

One day in the summer of 1988 when I went to the salon to get my hair cut, she announced that this would be her last time to service me as she was planning to move with her boyfriend to the Bahamas to open a beauty salon there.

One evening near the date she and her boyfriend were scheduled to fly to the Bahamas, I had a dream about her. I saw her face looking directly at me and she was crying hysterically. Sobbing uncontrollably, she screamed, "My boyfriend left me. He isn't with me and I don't know what I am going to do. Help me! I'm all by myself and I don't know what to do."

I responded very calmly and told her, "Don't worry, you are going to be all right. Calm down. You're okay; you're okay."

She began to stop crying and regained her composure but she was very concerned about her boyfriend not being with her. Since I didn't see any other images except her face in my dream, I didn't have the benefit of gathering additional information from the surrounding scenes. The only information I had was her face and how distraught she was.

I kept reassuring her that she would be all right and every time I did that, she seemed to calm down. I told her that she would soon be making a very big decision but that she was not to worry about making the decision. The decision that she would make would be the best decision for her and the right one.

She listened very intently to my words of wisdom. I told her not to worry about her boyfriend and that the decision she would make would be independent of her boyfriend. I also told her that she would find great strength within to choose the kind of life she wanted for herself.

At first she didn't believe that she had any strength because she was feeling very vulnerable and alone, but once again, I reassured her that deep within her was a part of herself that could take good care of her if she would simply trust it. She listened intently and began to feel more courageous and strengthened to make her important decision. Her face radiated confidence in place of the fear she experienced earlier. She thanked me for being there when she needed me. I told her I loved her and she would be fine.

I awoke from the dream in the morning and because so many of my dreams come true, I have learned through the years to listen to the feelings I experience upon waking. If the dream somehow speaks to my inner intuitive self and I am left with the feeling that the dream is true, then it usually is.

My feelings that morning spoke to my inner being in such a way. I knew that she was in trouble and I had great concern for her. I kept thinking about her and wondered if she made it to the Bahamas with her boyfriend safely or whether he may have abandoned her for some reason.

Several weeks later, I made an appointment with a new stylist in the same hair salon to have my hair cut. One of the first things I said to the new stylist was, "Did Sally make it to the Bahamas all right?"

There was no response. I continued. "I had a dream about her a few weeks ago and I dreamt that she got into some trouble. My dreams usually come true and I am concerned about her."

His reply was, "Yes, Sally did get into some trouble; I'll tell you all about it when I'm through cutting your hair."

After my hair was cut, he quietly led me into a private office and said, "I'm curious about your dream; tell me more."

So I told him the whole story. With a rather pained expression on his face, he then informed me that a few days prior to leaving for the Bahamas, she and her boyfriend were killed in an automobile accident. She died instantly, and her boyfriend clung to life for about one-half hour, and then he died.

Apparently, I was communicating with her as she was making her transition to the next life. Her concern for her boyfriend was obvious, but I am sure that they found one another as soon as he died. It makes me happy to know that our connections to other people continue to exist even after death. We can still continue to share the experience of journeying through parts of life and death together.

Goodbye, Dear Friend

This account is of a young man who committed suicide in 1989. He was a dear friend of my family and was very distraught over the death of his father who had died years earlier. Unaware of Austin's death on the night of his suicide, I had a dream about him. In the dream, I was walking into his bedroom where he was sitting. The moment he saw me his eyes lit up, and he bolted from his chair embracing me with a big bear hug.

"Nancy," he said, "Thank you so much for being such a good friend to me all these years. I love you very much. You always loved me so unconditionally, and I want you to know how much I treasured that kind of love."

I was so touched by his sweet words and tenderly looking into his eyes, I said to him, "You were like a son to me so it was easy to love you so much."

Austin replied, "No, your love was pure love. Your love was so special and so are you."

We hugged again and then he said, "I have to go now and go back to where I live."

Instantly, I was confused because the scene was taking place in the bedroom of his home, and I thought he was mistaken somehow. He immediately read my thoughts and said, "No, this is not where I live any longer."

He pointed upward and when I looked up, the roof of his house was missing. I could see the vast universe with the stars and planets shining so brightly above.

"That's where I live now," he said.

With a deep, intuitive understanding, I knew that he was telling me the truth and that soon he had to leave. I told him that I understood and that it was okay if he had to leave. At least we were sharing a loving moment together and telling one another how deeply our lives had touched one another. We both felt tremendous joy in communicating our love for one another. Suddenly, after our last hug, he "flew" upward into the dark universe above and I watched him fade away. I felt at peace. The dream ended.

The next morning, the feelings that the dream imparted were very strong. My immediate reaction was to call him on the telephone and see how he was, but a few hours later, his family called and told me that he had committed suicide **in his bedroom** during the night.

A Mother's Love

"And it came to me, and I knew what I had to have before my soul would rest.

I wanted to belong to my mother. And in return I wanted my mother to belong to me."

—Gloria Vanderbilt

My mother and I had a very close relationship with one another. She was the wind beneath my wings, and when she was dying in the hospital of cancer, I had a vivid experience a few hours before her death. To preface that experience, I need to point out that my mother had been telling her children for years that she didn't want to die and leave her children, even though we were all grown men and women. Her love for her children was beyond words.

She was suffering excruciating pain one evening and nearly collapsed, so my brothers and I immediately took her to the hospital where they admitted her. We left the hospital not knowing that after we left, the doctor put her into an induced coma to relieve her excruciating pain. When we arrived at the hospital the next morning, mother was comatose, unable to speak or move. We never had the chance to talk to her again. Because she was terminal, the doctors discontinued all attempts to keep her alive. We were told that she would die within the week.

Mother held on to life for two weeks. I stayed at her bedside around the clock, taking short 15 minute naps in the doctors' lounge. My brothers kept me company. The doctor approached me one evening and told me to go home and sleep.

"No!" I said. "I don't want to leave my mother."

He pleaded with me, "You need to sleep, otherwise you are endangering your own health. You have been here for two long weeks and you need a good night's sleep. Go home and you can come back in the morning." Reluctantly, I heeded his advice and went home to sleep.

At three o'clock in the morning, I woke up suddenly and sat up in bed, **fully awake**. In front of my eyes and at ceiling level, I saw a large red heart. It appeared to be stuffed, like a pillow, thick and soft. The edges of the heart were tattered and torn as if the heart was being ripped apart. Immediately, I knew somehow in the depth of my own heart that my mother was communicating to me that her heart was breaking because she had to leave me. She was reaching out to me from her coma to bring me her final love in a form that I would relate to.

She always knew that I had extraordinary abilities that allowed me access to other-worldly dimensions. I used to have long conversations with her about some of the experiences I had, and I remember telling her about some of the after-death communications I had received from people who had died. She was skeptical, but I insisted that these communications were not only possible, but trustworthy.

"Mother, when you die, will you please bring me a message?" I asked her one day.

She shrugged her shoulders a bit, and with a bit of hesitation, she said, "Okay."

I had a very hard time falling back to sleep after that vision of the red heart. I was so filled with the love that my mother was bringing to me from the depth of her dying heart. Love casts out fear, so I cannot say that I felt any fear whatsoever. Like osmosis, her heart had entered into my own heart and we became one, entwined with the unconditional love that death cannot undo.

When early morning came, my brothers and I rushed to the hospital and were told that our mother died moments before our arrival.

These accounts of deceased loved ones wanting to bring us a message from the beyond confirms the veil connecting the physical realm with the spiritual realm is a thin one. It confirms the fact that love knows no barriers and that love is stronger than death itself. The spirit of love is eternal and never dies. The spirits of our loved ones know the reality of the continuity of life and have a clear vision that love is eternal. Time and space are no deterrents to eternal love and communication with our loved ones for there is no separation in spirit. All live in divine spirit whether it is in this world or the world beyond.

Recalling those memories of after-death communications that took place years before Ched died were especially comforting to me. There's no more powerful factor that can be grasped than the sheer astonishment of finding out that our loved ones can still communicate with us from beyond the grave. My experiences in this regard have allowed me to remain open to the possibility that Ched would contact me in some way following his own death. He didn't disappoint me.

9

Yellow Roses

"The sweetest flower that blows, I give you as we part.
For you it is a Rose, For me it is my heart."

—Frederick Peterson

April 28, 2011

It had only been six weeks since my husband died. My mind, heart, and soul were still in a state of shock along with the feeling of being engulfed in a deep, bottomless pit of anguish. April 28th would have been our 49th wedding anniversary. I felt I needed to honor that day, the day that heaven joined us together as husband and wife so many years ago. I wanted to honor my husband's spirit as well, so I decided to put my grief aside for that day and plan an anniversary dinner for the two of us. I bought one small five-ounce lobster tail, which I haven't had in years, some fresh green beans and a salad along with our favorite white wine.

Ched always bought me yellow roses for our anniversary and special occasions because they are my favorite flowers. I decided that our anniversary dinner should also include a bouquet of yellow roses as a symbol of his love for me so I searched all over town for some. I couldn't find any. Disappointed, I went to

WalMart and purchased one thirty-inch long-stemmed artificial silk yellow rose. Not the real thing, but I figured it would serve the purpose.

When I was transferring the items I purchased into my car, the yellow rose was not there. Where did it go? I bought it; I had the receipt for it. I thought perhaps it blew out of one of the bags, but heck, I would have seen it since the cart was in front of me. I looked all around the adjacent parked cars but the rose wasn't to be seen. I went back to the check-out counter and asked the cashier if I left the yellow rose there but he told me I didn't. Where did it go?

Now I was really disappointed. I was resigned to the idea that the yellow roses that my husband loved to give me on our anniversary wouldn't be on the dinner table that evening. As I was leaving the parking lot at WalMart, I suddenly heard a voice in my head saying, *Nancy, go to Aldi's, that small grocery store just around the corner. Buy some red peppers.*

Why in the world would I think of doing that? I wondered? I didn't need red peppers, but I went to the store anyway. I can't explain it, but it was as if I were being directed to go to that store for a purpose, and it wasn't for red peppers.

I bought some red peppers and an avocado and proceeded to the check-out counter. At the counter was a display of fresh flowers for sale. In the middle of the pack was a bouquet of six yellow roses smiling up at me as if my husband were saying, *"I love you Nancy."*

Many of us tend to doubt and deny aspects of experiences that aren't verifiable. We are prone to dismiss these events by saying, "Oh, it's just a coincidence." But for the person experiencing this phenomenon it is very significant and meaningful.

For me, the events that took place with the yellow roses is an example of synchronicity, and I believe, a way that my husband communicated with me to make sure I had REAL yellow roses for our anniversary. Ched had always insisted that I had fresh yellow roses when he was alive. He would special order them from the florist weeks in advance to make certain I would have them. He detested, I mean really hated artificial flowers of any kind. When I bought that single yellow artificial rose at WalMart, I knew Ched must have been blowing a fuse! I could hear his voice inside my head scolding me for buying it and saying he would NEVER buy me artificial yellow roses! Somehow that artificial yellow rose disappeared and I was led by the voice in my head to the one place that had the REAL yellow roses waiting for me to pick them up and place them on our anniversary dinner table.

For dinner, I set a place for my husband's spirit to sit with me. I played some soft music in the background from a CD called "Music of the Angels." Appropriate, right? We had a lovely candlelight dinner, the REAL yellow roses and some nice conversation about how wonderful a marriage we had together. No, I didn't hear his audible voice of course, but I knew his spirit was with me. I felt his love, or I wanted to so much. When he was still alive, at the end of our daily dinners, Ched would pick up my hand and kiss it to thank me for the nice dinner, so I put my hand out for his spirit to kiss and I felt loved again.

Yellow Roses Again!

The date was April 28, 2012 which would have been our 50th wedding anniversary. We were going to renew our wedding vows, but of course Ched died one year earlier. But I decided to renew my promise to love him for eternity, a vow that honored a lifetime of the cherished love I have for him.

The previous year on our anniversary as you recall, I received the yellow roses through synchronicity and absolutely knew that Ched had a part in bringing them to me. I prayed that Ched would bring me a sign for our 50th anniversary date. The following story describes the answer to my prayers.

I have a dear friend who lives in New Jersey who I never met but I love her very much. Her name is Josie Varga. She is an author who is interested in sharing the good news about after-death communications and life beyond death. Since we are both authors interested in the same subject, we often email one another and have become dear friends.

About a week before Ched's and my special anniversary date, Josie emailed me and asked me for my mailing address as she wanted to send me something. I replied to her email and gave her my address and didn't think much of it. Later that week, I emailed her about something and happened to mention that Ched and I would have celebrated our 50th wedding anniversary in a few days, had he lived.

On April 28th, a very emotional day for me, I had been praying for a sign from Ched. I browsed through our wedding album admiring how youthful we looked as we began our new life together as man and wife. I think I recalled every detail of that day so I would never forget it. We had promised to love and care for one another until "death do us part" and now that reality had come to pass. I cried a lot because I missed him so much. I cried because we were unable to renew our wedding vows like we had planned to do.

All the memories of the past were pouring into and out from the hole in my heart. Yet I knew Ched was okay. Because of my Heavenly experiences, I knew he was filled with love, joy, and peace unspeakable, yet it did not soothe the raw emotion of the pain that separation had created for me. I ached to receive a message from him.

I called out to him in my anguish. "Ched, where are you? I need to know you are with me on our anniversary. I need you to bring me a message. Please bring me a message! God, please allow Ched the ability to bring me a message."

But the day was coming to a close. It was 5:00 pm already and nothing had happened.

Knock, knock. Someone was at the front door. I had a lung virus for weeks and I looked like a distressed hag, but I answered the door. A very handsome young man in a beautiful navy bluesuit was carrying an arrangement of 13 beautiful long-stemmed YELLOW ROSES in a vase of water! As he handed the arrangement to me he said, "Happy Anniversary."

I was anxious to see who sent those beautiful yellow roses to me so I quickly read the card.

It said: "Dear Nancy, these roses are not from me; they are from Ched. Happy Anniversary with all his love. I heard a voice telling me to buy you yellow roses. Please call me and I will explain. Love you, Josie"

I broke down sobbing from happiness that filled every crevice of my heart. I immediately called Josie and she explained that one day she heard a voice in her head telling her to "buy Nancy yellow roses." She said it stunned her. "Why?" she wondered. She had no idea why she was supposed to buy me yellow roses, someone she never met! She told her husband about the voice in her head telling her to "buy Nancy yellow roses," but she didn't understand why she should do this. She asked her husband what she should do and he told her to go ahead and buy them. So the next thing Josie did was to email me and ask me what my address was. She didn't tell me why she wanted my address and I didn't ask.

Remember, Ched contacted Josie to tell her to buy me yellow roses BEFORE she knew my anniversary was coming up. She listened to that voice in her head and made a decision to buy them for me without knowing why. She never met me and never met Ched. It was several days after she asked for my address that I told her of the anniversary.

I can only imagine how Josie must have felt when she realized that Ched's spirit had contacted her about the yellow roses before she even knew about the important anniversary. She must have been overjoyed to have been an instrument of love from Ched to me. One day I hope to meet Josie and give her a hug of appreciation for listening to that prompting in her head and acting upon it to bring me those yellow roses from Ched. She could have easily dismissed that voice in her head, but thank God, she didn't.

It was 45 degrees outside on that cold, rainy day in April. Even though I had a bad virus for three weeks I donned a warm coat and gently pulled one long-stemmed yellow rose from the arrangement Josie sent. I gathered Ched's photo, my heart-shaped necklace that contains some of Ched's ashes, his wedding ring, my Bible and a new ring that I would use to renew my vow to love him for eternity. I walked to the memorial garden my son and I created for him and I sat on the bench seat under the white birch tree he loved so much. The wind whistled through the tall ash trees and the chilly mist perched on my eyeglasses but I was warmed by the love I was feeling for Ched and for the sign he brought me on our Golden Anniversary to let me know his love was and is still with me.

Before I left, I thanked God for the amazing gift I received that day knowing that love never dies and that even in death, there is a way for our loved ones to touch our lives in a way that even in death, defies our understanding. The universe is filled with love and when we tap into it, we become transformed by it. I know that happened to me that day.

What makes this message from Ched so awesome is that he was a full-blown skeptic on the subject of life after death. Before he died, I told him to be sure and bring me a message from the other side. He responded by saying, "If there is no life after death, then I won't be able to bring you a message, and then you will be wrong and I will be right."

I replied, "You will see that you will live again after you die, so be sure to bring me a message."

Well, I think we now know who is right and who was wrong. I'm so happy he found out for himself that life after death exists and that he was able to bring me that message after all in a way that was especially meaningful to me.

The moral of this story is that love never dies. Love between souls who shared a physical life together continues to exist after death. The mystery of the afterlife cannot be understood, only welcomed into the sacredness of the human heart where it can continue to nourish and instill the "peace that passeth all under-standing."

In the meantime, I will continue to write and speak to witness to the mystery of the unseen in the hope that others will be inspired to understand there is more to our reality than meets the eye. When we are ready to embrace that awareness, the universe will open to us and bring us what we seek.

September's Yellow Roses

Ched, his two brothers and sister always celebrated their family reunions every year. Some reunions were trips, others were spent at a sibling's house for a weekend. When Ched was no longer able to travel due to ill health, some of the family reunions were spent at our house. A few months after Ched died, I received a phone call from Ched's brother asking me if they could have their family reunion at my house in September, 2012. What could I say? I said okay, but I was still reeling from the heart-wrenching pain of Ched's death. How would I be able to host their family reunion without my beloved Ched at my side? How would I deal with their laughter, their stories, and not hearing Ched's laughter intermingled with theirs? Oh how I would have loved to hear Ched's stories again even after hearing them a hundred times before; but his voice was forever silenced in the storeroom of my memories. I was not looking forward to this family reunion without Ched being part of it, his voice and his laughter missing, a heartache unbearable.

"Ched," I cried out into the silence of my surroundings, "You better be here when your family comes for their reunion. I need you here with me!"

I talk to Ched every single day. It brings me comfort and I feel close to him that way. No, I'm not crazy. I'm just still crazy in love with him, that's all!

In the Spring of 2011 when he died, I planted two yellow rose bushes outside my kitchen window so I could always be reminded of Ched's love for me in the way he always brought me yellow roses for special occasions. But in the summer of 2012, I noticed the two rose bushes developed a disease and they were having their own near-death experiences. I cut the rose bushes almost to the ground hoping to renew their strength and save their precious lives. Slowly, they revived with the growth of new leaves, but as summer was nearly over, the odds of having roses bloom again that year was almost nil.

Days before Ched's family arrived for the reunion, I noticed one, single bud beginning to form on each yellow rose bush. On the day when everyone arrived, each of those buds burst into full yellow roses! It was Ched's way of telling me he was going to be present with all of us for the family reunion that weekend after all.

My birthday arrived one week later, September 23rd. Once more, a single yellow rose appeared in full bloom on each rose bush not one day earlier, and not one day later, but on my birthday! I cut the roses from the rose bushes and placed them in a lovely vase in the kitchen so I could see them and smell their sweet fragrance every time I passed by.

Sometimes when I am walking through the rooms of the house in the dead of winter with snow falling softly to blanket the ground outside, the scent of roses suddenly fills the house. There are no roses in the house at that time, only their fragrance filling my nostrils and reminding me that Ched is near. With my eyes closed, I breathe in the delicious scent of his love, his proximity close to me. The scent of the roses is often times short-lived, just long enough to catch my attention to let me know that Ched is near.

How is this possible? Am I reading too much into this? Is this simply a coincidence? No. Yellow roses were always Ched's way of bringing me his love so tenderly in the form of the beautiful roses that I loved so much. Love knows no boundaries, no distance. No one can understand the mysteries of the universe, but I am so grateful that I can receive its gifts without having doubts about them.

Dreams

One of the most common golden bridges that bereaved people experience is to dream of their deceased loved one. It was shortly after Ched died that he appeared to me in a dream. It was the evening before I was hosting an annual summer party for friends a few months following Ched's death. Even though I was in the throes of full-blown grief, I wanted to have my dear friends with me for this summer gathering. Ched had always looked forward to these gatherings even though his illness prevented him from being part of it for long hours. He usually retired to his bed after he became too weak to socialize any longer.

In my dream, Ched was sitting at the kitchen table awaiting the arrival of my friends for the party that would commence in just a few hours. He was smiling at me and he looked **so happy**. He was looking forward to seeing everyone again. He was also talking to me, but I could not hear what he was saying. I also noticed that there was a vase filled with yellow roses centered on the kitchen table where he was sitting.

When I awoke from my dream, I knew that Ched was communicating to me that he would be present with all of us at the party that day. The yellow roses that were on the kitchen table were a sign of his love for me, a gift coming from his heart to mine from beyond the earthly dimension.

When the guests arrived and we were seated on the screened-in porch enjoying our food and wine, I told them about the dream I had the night before, and I told them that Ched was surely with us in spirit enjoying our company. We all raised our glasses to toast Ched and welcomed him. As I watched my friends' smiling faces acknowledging Ched's spirit with us, a warm feeling swept over me. I imagined it to be a silent hug from Ched.

A few weeks after the party, I purchased some artificial yellow silk roses that look very life-like, and I placed them in the center of my kitchen table. Everyone who sees them thinks they are real. The yellow roses remind me that Ched's love is everlasting, just like the everlasting yellow roses that he placed on the kitchen table for me during my dream.

I have had other visits from Ched during my dreams and somewhere in my dream there is always a yellow rose to signify that I can rely on that dream to be a real visitation from him.

Every night before I fall asleep and every morning as soon as I wake up, I say these words without fail. "Goodnight Ched; I love you." Upon waking I say, "Good morning Ched; I love you."

During one dream, Ched handed me a yellow rose and said, "Good night Nancy; I love you too." Wow! Following that particular dream, I became so aware that he watches over me, even as I sleep. When I awake, I am comforted to know that he begins his day with me, and I begin my day with him. We are never apart.

Ched's love for me did not die with his physical body. His love remains with me through all the wonderful synchronicities that I am able to recognize. And by recognizing them, I give Ched the verification that I have received his love! His smile must be as wide as Heaven itself. Thank you, Ched, for giving me that message I asked you to send me before you died. You chose to do it in the form of yellow roses, a way that had personal meaning for both of us. Your message that you continue to live following your physical death and that your relationship with me continues, is now testimony to others who will learn the story of the yellow roses. Thank you Ched. THANK YOU!

10

I Imagine

"We must let go of the life we have planned, so as to accept the one that is waiting for us."

—Joseph Campbell

Mother's Day 2013

The hummingbirds returned from their long and arduous trip from Mexico to drink the sweet nectar I provide in their feeders. It is always a joy for me to welcome them along with the warm weather. As I was watching these amazing little creatures swooping down to drink the sugar water, I became aware of the lessons they have to teach me.

Hummingbirds are unique because they can fly backwards, teaching me that I can look back at my past, but not dwell there. They teach me that I can hover at times, giving pauses to my grief, and that I can continue to move forward.

During the night, hummingbirds are not able to maintain their normal body temperature so they go into a sort of temporary hibernation. Then when morning comes, they must eat quickly in order to rev up their metabolism again so they won't die. It is amazing that these tiny creatures live within just hours of death each and every day.

As I watched the hummingbird at my feeder, I thought how similar I was to it. My grief put me into a sort of hibernation phase from everyday life. It was a place of rest and recovery. But the hummingbird knows instinctively that when the light of day appears, it must "wake up" and begin to live a new day searching for the conditions that will keep its tiny body alive. I realize that I too, in time, will need to "wake up" from my own hibernation of grief and begin the search for my own daily sustenance.

I will still need to move forward slowly and surely, but having given grief its opportunity to unfold according to my own timetable, I realize that today the first rays of dawn are visible. The pain is not as intense as it once was. I have and will continue to allow myself room for that which I cannot see, hear, touch, or control, and I will attempt to bring the whole of myself to the people who care about me. But I must emphasize, I must give grief its time and go through it in my own way. No one can complete this painful journey for me. No one can "fix" me. I'm grieving as fast as I can!

I have come to see that Ched's presence in my life has not only continued beyond his death but has flowered and grown, as I have. I can finally see it. Ched had come for a reason and left when his time was over.

My life from this point on is uncertain, as everyone's life is. The best I can do is to have the faith that I can continue living without my beloved Ched at my side. I am comforted by finding ways of remaining connected internally with Ched in order to find a place for him in my current life, because remembering him honors him. Remembering him heals me. Remembering him creates the immense gratitude that is like the most wondrous salve for my wounded spirit. As long as I can keep his spirit alive in my heart, that bond of love we shared will always be my great teacher.

And as long as I can let myself remember the days we spent together, I believe it will be easier to "let go" and accept that those days are gone, but not forgotten. I still have to take baby steps to walk the path that will lead me to feel a sense of inner peace and acceptance. But I find in doing this, it is helpful for me to imagine all the different ways that Ched would be pleased with me as I move through my journey of grief and toward acceptance.

I imagine how pleased he must be to know that I recognize what a significant difference he made in my becoming the person I am today.

I imagine how proud of me he must be to see how many times I believed I couldn't handle my problems and discovered how much that helped me to grow.

I imagine he is with me to soothe my tears.

I imagine he is happy knowing that I look for the best in others as he did.

I imagine he understands that I have similar hopes and fears that all humans have, and that those needs will be met by other human beings who can love me and make my journey less lonely.

I imagine he is proud of me for the times I stood up for something I believed in – something that wasn't particularly popular, but assured the rights of someone less fortunate than me.

I imagine he is smiling when I say, "This is for you Ched," when I step out of the shower and mist myself with his favorite perfume.

I imagine he walks beside me when the sights and sounds of Mother Nature intuitively fill my body with light and love.

I imagine he is sitting in the passenger seat of the car whenever I drive somewhere and he is helping me to make good decisions about making left hand turns in a busy intersection as he always used to do for me.

I imagine he is happy that my cat Velcro has given me the gift of unwavering companionship and undying love.

I imagine Ched sits with me on the memorial bench seat by the white birch tree he loved so much.

I imagine he is happy that I am still able to do my gardening at my age and that I still enjoy doing it.

I imagine he is happy that I invite friends over for dinner parties.

I imagine he is proud of Chris and Randy to know they are keeping their promise to him to take good care of me after he died.

I imagine he is happy that I continue to love him so much.

I imagine he was pleased that his life on earth meant so much to so many people who loved him.

I imagine that he too, is on a journey in the afterlife that will advance his own soul's growth.

The pain and loss I have endured has led me on a new path for this journey of life and its lessons it has yet to teach me. I am being honest when I admit that I have mixed feelings of fear and avoidance of making changes. I realize that I am on the very edge of a place of uncertain possibilities. Making this transition requires faith that in order to empty and release myself from a life that supported my security, I will need to "let go" and allow my soul to gently guide me through the process of acceptance.

I realize I must try even though at times I want to scream, "I can't!" But at this stage in my journey through grief, I know I am making progress, small progress, but progress nevertheless. When Ched died, I felt that I too, wanted to die. This intense feeling of being disconnected from him after so many years as man and wife felt as if the center of my being was being tortured beyond what I was capable of surviving. I could not imagine that a day would come when those feelings would gradually subside, and I would begin to realize that there is still a beating heart at that center-that I am still alive.

His death is forcing me to learn how to respect my own decisions and how to go on in the face of what feels like unbearable loss. Surely, it is up to me to claim what dreams can be fashioned into reality, and what values I will continue to hold true to as I am being guided into a new chapter in my life. But while I will still have to weather the storms of loneliness, I will also know that Ched's spirit will stay nearby, mercifully allowing me to remember him with love instead of sorrow. We were bound together on our walk through life, but we were never meant to share all of life together, only to mark its passages.

I think of what my life would have been without Ched, had we not had the chance to give each other so much, and I realize that our time together was too short. There were a multitude of things taken for granted, but we were always able to offer respect and give each other the benefit of the doubt. He was my teacher in so many ways, using his own life as an example. In the end though, he succeeded in helping me to understand that life is meant to be lived to the fullest.

Our sons still need their mother's unconditional love even if they are grown men. They still need to be part of the love that created them and I will not short-change them in any way. They are my blessings from God and from Ched, and our gift to the world.

I still need to continue to write and speak of what my Great Teacher, the Light of God revealed to me during my near-death and near-death-like experiences. I still have my life to live and I must make good use of that time remaining. But I will always hold Ched close to my heart until I see him once again in Heaven.

Every so often, when I look at Ched's photo, I will have a sudden urge to smile instead of an urge to cry. It is as if I am gaining the perspective to acknowledge the cherished bond between us – the love that is truly timeless. It is during those moments that I can feel as if he is wrapping his spirit's arms around me alleviating my momentary heartache.

From the depths of my heart, I know that Ched wants me

to heal my sorrow. He wants me to celebrate him and remember him the way he was, and not the way he died. I hear his voice in my head encouraging me to "wake up" and smell the yellow roses of the life that lies ahead for me. I will do that in my own way and in my own time, but when that happens, *I will imagine that he is looking down upon me with his loving smile, whispering encouraging thoughts in my ear, the words he always used to say to me whenever he was proud of me, "That's my girl!"*

I am learning valuable lessons and they are ones that I will carry with me until my final day on earth. One morning I heard the loud, familiar shrill sound of the emergency squad racing toward my neighbor's house in the woods in the back of my house. I have known my neighbors since 1972 when we moved into our home. They too, had been high school sweethearts and had married at a young age.

John was now 80+ years old and had developed Alzheimer's disease. His wife Sara, decided to care for him at home as long as possible before moving him to a nursing home. He was in the latter stage of the disease; his muscles were beginning to forget how to work properly.

When I heard the emergency squad's siren, I was reminded of the many times the squad came for Ched. They came so often that they knew us by our first names. But now they were coming for John.

Oh no! Is this the day that John will die? Is this the day that Sara will have to place John in the nursing home? Is he going to be alright? I wondered. My concern for both of them was very great so I immediately started praying for both of them. Throughout the day and night they were in my prayers.

The phone rang at 6:00 pm; it was Sara calling to tell me what happened earlier in the day.

"Nancy, I knew you would be alarmed when you heard the emergency squad coming for John so I wanted to let you know what happened." She said.

"Yes, Sara," I said. "When I saw the squad driving down your driveway into the woods, I immediately started praying for the both of you. I was very concerned." I listened to her whimper a soft cry.

Sara told me that John's legs could not hold him up as he tried to get up and he fell onto the floor. She couldn't get him back on his feet again so she called the squad for help.

As she was talking, her voice became wrought with the uncertainty of what was in her future. I recognized her fear; I went through that fear with Ched but I refrained from saying, "I know how you feel Sara." I remember how those few words affected me when someone said those words to me. No, I couldn't possibly know how Sara felt; only she knew how she felt. She was experiencing her own thoughts, her own reactions to the events she was confronted with. Instead, I cried with her. I allowed my tears and my words to let her know that she was being loved and cared for, and that I was supporting her in a way that was not condescending.

The next morning I was watering my flowers in my garden when I saw Sara walking up to me.

"Nancy, I had to stop by and tell you how much all your words meant to me yesterday," as she approached me with open arms ready to hug me.

"I meant every word Sara, because my heart entwined with your heart as we were speaking," I said.

Our long hug was a genuine, heart-felt hug and she softly cried, knowing that my arms were open to her to absorb some of the pain she was feeling.

She told me that I understood what she was going through because of what I went through with Ched. I told her that I could not possibly understand what she was going through, only she knew that. But I did acknowledge that I empathized with her heartache.

As if she understood what I was saying, she said, "Many people are telling me that John will be alright and that I shouldn't worry so much. My minister told me that this is God's will and that I should accept this."

"How does that make you feel when people say those things to you?" I asked.

She seemed hesitant to confide in me and just shrugged her shoulders a little, so I asked that question again, telling her it was okay to talk to me about this.

"Well, I didn't like those comments," she replied sheepishly, as if it were wrong to think like that.

"Why?" I asked, knowing that by confiding in me it would allow her to bring to the surface her honest feelings rather than suppressing them. This understanding was yet another lesson I learned during my grief process. It is healthier to be real than to hide one's feelings, whatever those feelings may be.

"For one thing Nancy," she said. "John will not be alright. He is getting worse. There is no cure for his disease. He is going to die from it. And, I don't believe Alzheimer's disease is God's will. If it were God's will, then God is very cruel, isn't He? This is a terrible disease and what did John do to God that he deserved to suffer like this? He is a good man and he loves God." She cried, and I immediately wrapped my arms around her to let her know that in that moment, she was being loved in the midst of her tears and heartache.

Intuitively, I knew that I was giving Sara the support she needed. I learned through my own grief that people do not want patronizing words they think will be helpful, people need love, pure and simple. A hug without words is like a sponge absorbing some of the pain that someone is feeling at that moment.

Sara and I shared a connection that I believe, was honest and loving – two things that meant so much to the both of us. She thanked me for being a good friend to her and her hug felt like it was genuine love for me. I felt it; I knew it in my heart and soul. She went on her way, back to John to continue caring for him. As I watched her in the distance, I silently said a prayer to God asking to bring her the strength to move through her own journey of grief when that day comes. And when that day comes, I will be there for her with my arms open to embrace her heart and her pain.

I won't try to fix her. I will know that she is grieving as fast as she can.

About the Author

Nancy Clark is a national award-winning author, speaker and researcher. A cytologist by profession (study of cells), she is now retired and devoting her life to writing and speaking about spiritually transformative experiences. Having had such experiences personally, she is passionate about inspiring others to know that we are immortal spiritual beings gifted with a Divine inner nature that encourages us to live our authentic loving selves.

She is the president of the Columbus, Ohio International Association for Near-Death Studies, a chapter of (IANDS), member of The Academy for Spiritual and Consciousness Studies, Inc., and member of the National League of American Pen Women, Inc.

Nancy is interested in your comments. Please feel to contact her by email and she will reply as time permits.

Website: www.freewebs.com/nancy-clark

Email: nancyclarkauthor@gmail.com

Resources

Alexander, Eben. *Proof of Heaven*. New York: Simon & Schuster, 2012.

Association for Death Education and Counseling (ADEC). www.adec.org

Attig, Thomas W. *How We Grieve: Relearning the Old*. New York: Oxford Univ. Press, 1996.

Atwater, PMH. *Beyond the Light*. North Carolina: Transpersonal Publishing, 2009.

Bereavement and Hospice Support Netline. www.ubalt.edu/www/bereavement

Biebel, David B. *If God Is So Good Why Do I Hurt So Bad?* New York: Novpress, 1989.

Center for Loss and Life Transition. www.centerforloss.com

Christison, Kathleen. *It's All Right, I'm Only Crying: A Chronicle of Love & Grief*. Texas: Virtual Bookworm Publishing, 2012.

Compassionate Friends, Inc. www.compassionatefriends.org

Crisis, Grief and Healing. www.webhealing.com

Death and Dying Grief Support. www.death-dying.com

Dossey, Larry. *Reinventing Medicine: Beyond Mind-Body to a New Era of Healing*. San Francisco: Harper San Francisco, 1999.

Eternea. www.eternea.org

Gates, Philomene. *Suddenly Alone: A Woman's Guide to Widowhood*. New York: Harper Collins, 1990.

Grief Net. www.griefnet.com

Guggenheim, Bill and Judy. *Hello From Heaven!* New York. Bantam Books, 1995.

Hospice Foundation of America. www.hospicefoundation.org

International Association for Near-Death Studies (IANDS). www.iands.org

Jackson, Edgar N. *The Many Faces of Grief*. TN: Abingdon Press, 1977.

Kircher, Pamela. *Love Is the Link: A Hospice Doctor Shares Her Experience of Near-Death and Dying*. New York: Larson Publications, 1995.

Kubler-Ross, Elisabeth. *Living with Death and Dying*. New York. Macmillan, 1982.

Kushner, Harold S. *When Bad Things Happen to Good People*. New York: Schocken Books, 1989.

LeShan, Eda. *Learning to Say Good-bye: When a Parent Dies*. New York: Macmillan, 1976.

Moody, Raymond. *Life After Life*. New York: Bantam Books, 1975.

Moody, Raymond and Dianne Arcangel. *Life After Loss: Conquering Grief and Finding Hope*. New York: Harper Collins, 2001.

Near-Death Experience Research Foundation. www.nderf.org

Price, John W. *Revealing Heaven: The Christian Case for Near-Death Experiences*. New York: Harper Collins, 2013.

Ring, Kenneth. *Heading Toward Omega: In Search of the Meaning of Near-Death Experiences*. New York: Morrow, 1984.

Ring, Kenneth, and Evelyn Valarino. *Lessons from the Light: What We Can Learn from the Near-Death Experience.* NH: Moment Point Press, 2000.

Ritchie, George. *Ordered to Return: My Life After Dying.* VA: Hampton Roads, 1998.

Siegel, Bernie. *365 Prescriptions for the Soul: Daily Messages of Inspiration, Hope, and Love.* CA: New World Library, 2003.

Varga, Josie. *Visits from Heaven.* VA: A.R.E. Press, 2009.

Widownet. www.widownet.com

Other Books by Nancy Clark

*Hear His Voice: The Light's Message For Humanity: Revelations
From a Woman Who Came Back From Heaven's Door Twice*

1st World Publishing, 2012

My Beloved: Messages From God's Heart To Your Heart
Infinity Publishing, 2008
CD Version: *My Beloved: Messages From God's Heart To Your
Heart*

Infinity Publishing, 2011

*Divine Moments: Ordinary People Having Spiritually
Transformative Experiences*

1st World Publishing, 2012

All books are available directly from the publishers, on
Amazon.com and other online retailers and can be ordered
from any brick and mortar bookstore.